The Story of
Moreton Hall

THE STORY OF
MORETON HALL

Michael Charlesworth

Quiller Press

First published in the UK in 2003
by Quiller Publishing Ltd

British Library Cataloguing-in-Publication Data
        A catalogue record for this book
        is available from the British Library

ISBN 1 904057 35 7

Printed in England by St Edmundsbury Press Ltd, Bury St Edmunds,
Suffolk

Quiller Publishing Ltd
Wykey House, Wykey, Shrewsbury, SY4 1JA, England
E-mail: info@quillerbooks.com
Website: www.swanhillbooks.com

CONTENTS

Foreword

M ichael Charlesworth, as an historian, makes it clear that his account of Moreton's first ninety years is not a 'history', yet it is Moreton's story, a colourful account of the ups and downs of a family school: a school founded by a family, a school that unashamedly promotes the virtues of community living.

I'm occasionally asked why I came to work at Moreton - and why after eleven years I'm still here. The only honest answer I can give to both parts of the question is that Moreton is a wonderful environment in which to live and work.

When I first came for interview to be Principal in 1991, I looked around the school and met senior girls. The buildings and grounds were fine – better than fine, actually – but it was the girls who sold the school to Paula and me as prospective parents.

We could see Sarah and Clare, our daughters, at Moreton – and we wanted them to turn out like the girls who showed us around the school with such good humour and pride.

Over the last decade or so Moreton has addressed a variety of issues to ensure the school's continued success.

The raising of the academic standards was our first priority – in a world where Mr Blair wishes fifty per cent of all school leavers to attend university, we must ensure that all our Sixth Formers can proceed to Higher Education should they wish.

The development of a house-based pastoral and tutorial system has been the mechanism employed to ensure appropriate monitoring of girls, welfare and academic progress.

The appointment of staff committed to the full life of a busy boarding school has been exceptionally important in raising standards inside and outside the classroom.

A sensible, knowledgeable and supportive board of Governors, ably led by Malcolm Mitchell, oversees strategy and its implementation.

Music, drama, sport, outdoor pursuits, Moreton Enterprises and so on almost ad infinitum could not flourish without the commitment of the staff – and not just the teaching staff. The administrative, catering and ground staff also contribute very positively to the creation of a busy and successful school.

And those staff, like the girls, convey a sense of fun in living and working at Moreton.

A final assessment of what makes Moreton 'Moreton' is the enjoyment of being part of a school where individuals can flourish with a shared sense of purpose, a relish for taking part in a wide variety of curricular and extra-curricular activities that bind staff and pupils together.

So Moreton may have gone up the academic tables since 'your day', but then in 'your day' or in 'my day' for that matter, there were no measurements of the success of a school other than a full roll and a sense of having fun whilst achieving things you never thought you could quite manage: these are still the criteria that really matter.

As we look forward to the school's centenary, our new Sixth Form boarding house rises on the site of the old tennis courts: fifty girls in ensuite rooms in the new Charlesworth House, its future built upon the foundations of the past!

Michael Charlesworth has conveyed so well the essential spirit of Moreton in his 'story'. I am proud to have become part of the Moreton story and honoured to be allowed to develop further the school as it enters its tenth decade.

Jonathan Forster
April 2003

PREFACE

My connection with Moreton Hall started more than fifty years ago when I was entangled with Bronwen Lloyd-Williams in one of her current enthusiasms, the Council for Education in World Citizenship. Since then I have been a Governor for a number of years and Chairman for some of them; my wife taught briefly at the school before we were married. In recent years I have continued to be in touch with the school through my former pupil, Jonathan Forster. Thus when he suggested that I might try and write a book for the ninetieth anniversary I happily accepted and have enjoyed the task of trawling through the records in order to relate the developing story.

This is not a history of the school as such. Deeper research than I have been able to make would be required for that: and indeed there are many years when records are scanty or non-existent. For instance, for many past years there were no existing lists of members of staff and numbers of girls in the school were not always recorded. I do not doubt that there are omissions and errors in what I have written.

I hope nonetheless that I have described the broad picture of a remarkable school, with all its ups and downs, from the eleven little girls who assembled in Oswestry in 1913 to the bustling activity of 301 girls today.

I am grateful for the help of Old Moretonians of different generations whom I have consulted; and grateful to Jonathan Forster for constant encouragement, to Hilary Prescott for help with the photographs and to Kath Mountford for typing the manuscript in what time she could find from her full time duties.

Michael Charlesworth
April 2003

The Story of
Moreton Hall

1 GENESIS

Before the First World War, John Jordan Lloyd-Williams had been Headmaster of Oswestry Grammar School. Sadly, ill-heath had reduced him to being an invalid by 1913 (he died in 1916). Thus the care of their large family of two sons and nine daughters devolved upon his wife, Ellen Augusta Crawley Lloyd-Williams, while he retired to a house in Cardiganshire.

Ellen Lloyd-Williams was a woman of considerable character, determined and energetic with not only a will to succeed but also to command – qualities which she passed on to most of her offspring. In 1913 she set up a small school in what had been a boarding house at Oswestry School called Lloran

House. There were eleven boarders including her three youngest children, the children of cousins and friends and two day girls. This was the origin of what was to be Moreton Hall.

Of the children of John and Ellen Lloyd-Williams, three were to play a major role at Moreton Hall. Their family consisted of:

Grace, who took a degree in French; she wrote French text books and was an examiner for the Welsh Board.

Jim was in the Indian Police, then Chief Constable of Montgomery and finally of Worcestershire.

Mary was the musician of the family and went to the Royal College of Music.

Letty trained as a nurse and was a school matron, working at different times at Shrewsbury, Eton, Harrow and at Moreton Hall.

Ellen was a linguist and worked abroad for much of her life as a translator in the Diplomatic Corps.

John became a solicitor. He was for some time in the Royal Flying Corps, then a Chief Inspector with the Metropolitan Police and finally Chief Constable of Cardiganshire.

Kitty became a doctor, worked in London as an anaesthetist (on which subject she wrote a book), became Dean of the Royal Free Hospital School of Medicine and was the first woman Dean of The Faculty of Medicine, London University.

Betty took a degree in history and married Baillie Brett of the Indian Civil Service in which he rose to be Chief Secretary to the Government of India. After his retirement they lived in Worcestershire.

Bronwen went to the Bedford College of Physical Training, became a journalist and returned to be Principal of Moreton.

Sylvia was a scientist and taught at Roedean School before becoming Headmistress of King Edward VI School, Birmingham.

Gwladys had poor health and was an invalid for much of her life.

Altogether the family were a formidable list of achievers. Both boys married but of the girls only Betty. A commentary perhaps on the fact that between the wars there were two million more women than men in the population after the casualties of the First World War.

Bronwen, Sylvia and Gwladys were all young enough to take part in the adventure of Lloran House where staff consisted of their elder sisters Grace and Mary, under the all seeing eye of their mother Ellen, who then and subsequently in this very family school was known as 'Aunt Lil'. There was also a German fraulein and the girls went to Oswestry School for science lessons. The school was successful and numbers increased. For a time there were two small boys on the roll – who bullied the youngest girls; one was Philip Yorke later owner of Erddig House.

Aunt Lil now took a great act of faith and successfully negotiated the purchase of Moreton Hall. In this she was helped by her two brothers, Sir William Vincent and Sir Hugh Vincent who gave good practical advice. Moreton Hall was built in the reign of Henry VIII – reputedly in 1527 – and had been refronted in the time of William and Mary, hence the Dutch architectural influence. It had originally been surrounded by a moat with a drawbridge. For fifty years the owner had been Edmund Burke-Wood, a barrister from Middlewich, and the purchase was made from his daughters, Mary and Gertrude Burke-Wood at a cost of £3500, the purchase including 'outbuildings and cottages, grounds, plantation and garden thereto belonging and four acres of land adjoining'. A somewhat puzzling clause allowed the vendors 'full and free right of way at all times hereafter and for all purposes and with or without horses, cattle, carts and carriages over and along the drive for themselves and their successors...'.

Thus in the aftermath of the war Moreton Hall was established in 1919 and was for twenty years guided and shaped by Aunt Lil. Her authority was innate and effortless. She did no teaching but her influence was all pervasive. Her Christian faith was unshakeable and she never missed taking morning and evening prayers. Sadly Parkinson's Disease took her in the late 1920s but, despite her shaking hands, she in no way ceased to dominate the school until her death in 1940. 'A frail old lady, dressed in severe grey tailored suit. Her profile was delicately chiselled, fine wrinkles on her quizzical face, shining white hair gathered in a small neat bun, sparkling piercing eyes that searched your soul. Beautifully manicured practical hands held the book from which she read to us – The King of the Golden River. I was more fascinated by herself than her reading.' So wrote a girl in 1936.

La Frigante – 1923.

Ellen Lloyd-Williams (1860-1940) with her grandson on her lap (second right), and her eleven children and in-laws at the wedding of her daughter Elizabeth. They are on the front lawn of Moreton Hall.

The three daughters who played major roles in the running of the school were Miss Grace, Miss Mary and Miss Bronwen. Grace was a gentle soul, vague and seemingly unpractical, though probably not as gullible as she sometimes seemed to the girls. She taught French but was the most erudite of the family and her lessons would often diverge into other academic subjects in which she was interested. She was dressed, winter and summer alike, in a strange totally individual costume consisting of a dark sleeveless dress of heavy tweed and loose matching jacket. Intensely superstitious, she never wore green; when the new moon was due she walked about the garden until she had safely seen it in the open and not, disastrously, through glass. There was a softness about her but her rather sleepy eyes missed little.

Miss Mary taught music, history and divinity but music was the centre of her life. She was small, neat and immaculate and had a fund of nervous energy. An excellent pianist, her first love was nonetheless the violin. She formed the Moreton Hall Music Society, with help from neighbouring adults, and their concerts, at the school in the afternoon and at Oswestry in the evening were great school events. She, if anyone, could be called the executive at the school; she was highly practical and did the shopping in her small green car, called the 'pea'. In her scarce leisure time she found peace and quiet in gardening.

Miss Bronwen taught English, dancing, games and gymnastics. Slim, brown-eyed, with fair skin and short cut hair of a ravishing dark auburn, she had an air of restless driving energy. Her English lessons were exciting and wide-ranging; her very presence seemed to raise the temperature. One pupil said that, though she might have her back to the door, she knew when Bronwen came in; she had a presence. A brilliant lacrosse player (she had captained Wales), she was also a good cricketer. Her teams took the field with the absolute expectation of winning; they generally did.

Life in the early days at Moreton was spartan and there were no luxuries. The girls froze in winter despite a number of open fires in most rooms. The electricity was produced by a most temperamental engine which frequently broke down. The food was certainly 'plain' and there was not a lot of it. Supper consisted of two slices of bread and butter and some thin cocoa or Bovril. Certain dishes became very familiar, prepared by Ma James, the cook, particularly Ichabod stew (the glory has departed) and Ma James's leg.

Saxe blue had been the school colour since Lloran House days. Now the girls wore blue tweed coats, black velvet collars, black velour hats with the school badge; and Cromwell shoes – the hallmark of Moretonians for many years. Blue djibbahs were everyday dress. Much loved and lived-in cloaks provided some protection from the winter elements. In the summer there were

Sweeney.

white dresses, cream coats, panama hats and beige stockings.

In the gardens was Sweeney who devoted more than thirty years of his life to the service of the school, a familiar figure to all, never, it seemed, without his pipe and dog. He died in 1954, working to the last at the age of ninety-one. Two other stalwart figures were Mr and Mrs Condé – did he really have some French aristocratic background as was rumoured? He was to be found in the stoke hole, often surrounded by mountains of Cromwell shoes which he cleaned. She would be in the laundry where all the clothes and sheets for the entire school were washed by hand. And there would be a flock of maids who slept at the top of the house.

Gradually as the school expanded other buildings on the estate were brought into use and two ex-Army huts were purchased. How delightful sometimes to retreat into the old barn which served as a retreat from the rigour of life and where one might get warm in the hay.

The strong Christian emphasis of the school stemmed from Miss Grace and Miss Mary, strangely enough the only two of the nine daughters who were outwardly practising Christians. Their beliefs were rock solid and religious instruction for their charges was a high priority, best illustrated by the Sunday routine. Those who were confirmed walked to Weston Rhyn church for early Holy Communion. The whole school walked in crocodile formation to Chirk for matins (later to Gobowen) and the Head Girl solemnly gave each girl one penny for the collection. Sermons were long in those days and were seldom tailored for the young so considerable ennui was built up, though, in small consolation, if one was near the heating pipes Cromwells might surreptitiously be removed and the feet warmed. After lunch there were divinity lessons taken by Miss Grace and Miss Mary and the collects were learned and the day's Bible readings explained. Then in the evening was the school service of evensong, an anthem and a sermon, the choir finishing the day's worship by processing

1927 Summer. 2nd left front row Kyffin Williams.

out singing the doxology. Sunday evenings were free! Whatever spiritual effect these Sunday observances may or may not have had, at least it gave the girls a familiarity with the beauties of the prayer book, the authorised version of the Bible and a rich knowledge of church music. For some too there was additional religious knowledge as it was the custom to punish malefactors by setting them to learn a psalm. It must have been a relief on Sunday nights when Miss Mary as usual came round the bedrooms to say a final prayer and to produce her bottle of sweets (to the disapproval of Matron). You got two if you had brushed your hair a hundred times.

If religious teaching and practice were the first priority, the second might be said to be the inculcation of good manners. From their earliest years girls were expected to have a mature social sense and to be able to talk easily to adults; giggling, blushing and shyness were absolutely discouraged. One was expected to explain the school to potential parents and to show them around. This was all made easier because of the family atmosphere which the school engendered from its earliest days; there was no enforcement of harsh discipline. You behaved well because that was expected of you and because that was the whole tone of the school family society. At the head was Aunt Lil, the family icon, and with you every day were Miss Grace, Miss Mary and Miss Bronwen. You received half a crown from Aunt Lil on your birthday. One of her repeated sayings was 'You're worth your weight in gold' – praise taken to heart and cherished. On meeting one girl of doleful countenance, Bronwen's reaction was 'You don't look very cheerful, darling, have a piece of cake'. Emphasis was laid on speaking clearly and using the English language properly. In later times there were long lists of prize-winners over many years at the competitions held by the English Speaking Board.

Probably the activity which most Moretonians would particularly remember in these years between the wars was music. This was not in any sense an 'extra' as in many schools. Everyone was involved: most played instruments and all sang. Miss Mary was a brilliant director. The choir went through the whole range of church music – Stanford, S. S. Wesley, Walmsley, Stainer and others. The summer concert was a real highlight and Ernest Read of the Royal College of Music would come for the final rehearsals. Major works would be given – the Messiah, the St Matthew Passion, Hiawatha's Wedding Feast, with outside help from local singers. Visiting artists frequently came to give recitals – Solomon, Jelly D'Aranyi, Eileen Joyce; later Peter Pears and Benjamin Britten. At Parents' Weekend there would be ballets in which the whole school, regardless of shape or size would take part. Bronwen was a brilliant choreographer and under her inspiring leadership remarkable results were achieved, weaving dances from a Mozart symphony or the Franck Variations for instance and once when Eric Cundall conducted, the Polovtsian dances from Prince Igor. At the piano for many years was Mrs Unsworth who seemed able to sight read anything, while a wide range of costumes were made in school. In 1930 the gym was considerably enlarged, giving improved performance space; in order to pay for some splendid velvet curtains Bronwen sold her horse 'Freckles'. The music was not limited to Moreton for performances were given at Chirk Castle, at the Orthopaedic Hospital, at Weston Rhyn and at fêtes or social occasions in the locality. Plays did not much feature. Bronwen's taste was for large scale drama and ballet. Long remembered by those present was a production of Milton's Comus on the grass by the mulberry tree with the audience on the tennis court below, the Attendant Spirit appearing with ethereal unexpectedness poised on top of the garden wall. Many Moretonians carried with them through life the wide variety of music, sacred and secular, to which they had been so thoroughly introduced.

Mrs Lloyd-Williams (Aunt Lil) in the early days at Lloran House.

The school prospectus stated very firmly NO EXEATS and it might be thought that the school was a rather isolated community in its delightful rural setting but in fact there were many visits and many visitors. Lacrosse had, from the earliest days, been a major activity under Bronwen's enthusiastic direction. Every Saturday there were matches and teams travelled widely – to Penrhos, Huyton College, Lowther College, Queen's Chester and to distant Howells, travelling over the Horseshoe Pass, often in wild weather, in two large taxis under the direction of a well-known character, Exuperius Pickering Powell. On one occasion when the taxis stuck, the application of Moreton cloaks under the wheels made forward motion possible. There were trips to art galleries in Birmingham and Liverpool; there were trips to concerts in Shrewsbury, Oswestry and Liverpool; and on occasion to see a play in Stratford.

TRIO – Patricia Morris (Mrs Thompson), Joy Wood (Mrs Friendly), Mercia Pollock (Mrs Mason)

The family atmosphere was underlined by visits from the various Lloyd-Williams sisters who treated Moreton as home; and occasionally Aunt Lil's two brothers came, Sir William back from service in India, who read W. W. Jacobs to the girls and enjoyed it so much that his audience had difficulty in following the story. A certain frisson went round the establishment when these visits took place – in a wholly female school. Part-time staff also came in, one particularly remembered was Miss Rice-Oxley who paid a weekly visit to teach art and craft and arrived on her motor cycle, which always created a minor sensation though much outdone by the Reverend Thursby Pelham who arrived on a 'combination' – a motor cycle and side car, wearing goggles and his cap the wrong way round, with his wife in the side car.

Saturdays were always looked forward to. There was swimming in the Oswestry baths; there was riding under the care of Captain Gaskell; there were elaborate picnics; there were cookery classes. On the first Saturday of the winter term the whole school went blackberrying. In the evening there was dancing to gramophone records – the old 78s; or there might be a talk. Old Lord Trevor of Bryncyllte could always be deployed to give his well-known talk on the Annexation of the Cook Islands. In later years home clothes could be worn, natural nail polish applied, face powder liberally used and thus turned out the VIth form were allowed to visit Oswestry.

Numbers went up gradually between the wars. By 1935 there were about seventy girls; and occasionally there were briefly small boys in the bottom form. One of these was Kyffin Williams, the well-known artist, and certainly the most distinguished Old Moretonian. He came from his home in Chirk in a dog cart with a posse of day girls who disapproved of the small boy and he was made to sit on the floor of the cart. Boys tended to be quarrelsome. One Old Moretonian remembers being in the bottom form which consisted of two boys and two girls; civil war was constant; once she was thrown into the Ha Ha among the nettles. But much later meeting her tormentor by chance on a train, they made up their differences; more than that – at a later stage – they got married.

In 1935 Bronwen decided that Moreton was too small a stage for her and took off for London and the big world. She became a freelance journalist, went to the Spanish Civil War to report for the Quakers, was in Czechoslovakia and, when war came, was in London during the Blitz. But she came down to Moreton every Saturday if she was in the country and continued her dance productions – a weekly injection of creative energy. Thus through the 1930s Moreton continued to be a family school. Other staff of course there were but few stayed long enough to make a lasting impression. 'Mamselles' came and went; French accents improved but there was a marked reluctance to sit at the

'Play up and play the game' – Cricket team: pre-war.

'French table' at lunch. There was no laboratory and no science was taught though there were some biology lessons from part-time staff for girls who aimed at being doctors. One person however seemed permanent, Dr Charles Salt, medical officer for forty years and guide, philosopher and friend to all. On Sunday evenings he gave art lectures. Another regular member of the community was Ross, the great Irish wolfhound, who lay about in inconvenient places and was liable to snap at your heels.

As in all schools at that time, there were frequent outbreaks of disease when those affected would be isolated and sheets soaked in Lysol were hung in the passages. In 1933 an outbreak of measles meant that twenty-five girls had to stay in school for Christmas. They were rewarded by a splendid Christmas dinner which one participant remembers as being the first time she saw finger bowls being used. Such are the details which often stick in the mind. Then there were occasional national events which impinged on the school. The death of the King (George V) was one such when on every evening between his death and funeral, the girls sang a litany upon their knees followed by 'Lest we forget...' by Kipling.

Aunt Lil died in 1940; almost to the end she attended prayers every day, sitting upright in her cane chair. She had become increasingly frail. On one quiet Saturday afternoon a girl heard cries of distress from the staff bathroom. She ran to fetch Miss Mary who climbed a ladder to get through the bathroom window to find Aunt Lil, unable to move, almost submerged by the rising water.

1938 Lacrosse Team.

She died in the knowledge that she had created a remarkable school with its own ethos on which she had placed the unmistakable Lloyd-Williams stamp. Despite the spartan conditions, Moretonians recalled with gratitude the care of the staff, the warmth of friendships and achievements in various spheres. They recalled too the little traditions built up over the years – the annual carol service in the Hall at Christmas time, the log fire blazing, the girls with their rugs sitting on the floor in their pyjamas consuming mince pies, claret cup and nuts. Then there was the advent wreath decorated with apples and candles which hung in the Hall: Cocked Hat Sunday when the most ingenious hats were created: and Ivy Sunday – the last of the term – when the whole school was decorated with ivy. There were too, illegal midnight feasts in bedrooms, preceded by out-of-bounds dashes to a shop to obtain provender; and Hallowe'en was always celebrated.

One Old Moretonian, looking back, said that the three things she took away from Moreton were a sense of religion, an appreciation of music and a code of behaviour and good manners. Aunt Lil would have been well satisfied with that epithet.

11 WAR AND AFTER

The coming of the Second World War in 1939 did not greatly disturb the running of the school but, because it was in a safe area, it did lead to a considerable increase in numbers, some girls coming from a school in Switzerland in 1940 when the Germans over-ran most of Europe. Accordingly Miss Grace took the junior girls to Henlle Hall which was situated on the other side of Holyhead Road; some facilities were shared but it was in effect a separate school.

Miss Mary was now in charge and certainly gave that impression, striding round the school in her tweeds with the long gold chain around her neck with which Moretonians of the day always associated her. There were, as everywhere, the restrictions and the shortages of wartime. The blackout was operated by Condé who put up the necessary boards every night on the insides of which the girls drew some spirited murals. There were air raid shelters but it was very infrequently that they were used, though the drone of bombers going over to bomb Liverpool were at one time heard nightly. Moreton did not suffer too badly as regards rationing of food, the country location being an advantage. Neighbouring Park Hall was greatly expanded as a military training camp which sometimes brought high-class entertainment to the Garrison Theatre where Moretonians saw the Vic-Wells ballet, with Robert Helpmann, and heard a John Gielgud recital. That was some consolation to the domestic tasks which war brought with it, such as potato picking and beet singling.

By the end of the war there were one hundred girls in the school. The staff had been increased. Two who were to make enormous contributions to the school were Miss Edwards and Miss Inskip. The former took charge of the music from Miss Mary. She was wholly devoted to the direction of the orchestra, of the choir and her pupils. Miss Inskip was an outstanding pianist and a skilled accompanist to ballets, choirs and operas. Both spent their whole working lives at Moreton. The remarkably high standard achieved is illustrated by the programme of the concert given in June 1945, the choir and orchestra

Unison.

drawing on not only Moretonians but boys from Gordonstoun (evacuated to Shropshire), Shrewsbury School and local friends. There was a movement of Schubert's 5th Symphony, movements from Mozart's Concerto for Two Pianos and Concerto for Three Pianos (all played by Moreton Girls), a Beethoven Concerto played by Rosalie Inskip and finally Mendelssohn's Elijah Part I. The conductor was Morgan Nicholas, a diminutive and energetic Welshman who was organist of Oswestry Parish Church and was a familiar and helpful figure at the school for twenty years. Thea Musgrave, to acquire later fame as a composer and performer, played in one of the concertos. She took her L.R.A.M. while at school – not a unique achievement but a very rare one.

Another who devoted her working life to the school was Doreen Campbell. She taught art, sewing and mending – the latter not to be despised in time of war shortage and coupons. She had a really outstanding talent for colour and design. In innumerable productions she designed, made and fitted costumes – and the scenery where necessary. Her Scottish thrift meant that nothing was wasted and the foundations were laid for the extensive dress room. She was also a housemistress with a strong dislike of unpunctuality and disorder. For a time Mildred Eldridge assisted in art lessons. She was married to the curate at Chirk who was R. S. Thomas, the poet. For many years Mrs Richards was in charge of science, vague yet immensely erudite, with a perpetual cigarette. She was a keen zoologist and botanist. For ten years Marion Halton Davis took a leading part in the daily running of the school, bringing much practical ability and experience into the administration as well as teaching English; and Moretonians of the war and post-war years will remember with affection 'Mamselle' – Marie Le Caer, who taught French for twenty-two years; did she really know General de Gaulle? At any rate she was a keen admirer of his.

Despite the war, school events continued as usual so far as possible. Parents' Weekend was held every summer, the Fathers' Cricket Match took place and there was the gymkhana. Miss Grace found Henlle Hall too small for the junior school and moved to Llantysilio Hall at Llangollen; meanwhile every possible space was used to fit in the increased numbers in the main school. A third 'sett', that is a division in the school for competitive purposes, was added and titled 'Vincents', joining Venables and Calverts. Emphasis on deportment was maintained as this excerpt from the Moretonian shows: 'As a whole the school sits up well at prayers and moderately well at meals but does not sit well in class or walk well. With increasing numbers the standard of deportment seems to be deteriorating. This is unfortunate as deportment used to be outstandingly good throughout the school. It is to be hoped that this high standard will soon be achieved again.' Nonetheless there were forty-three deportment stripe holders named.

Miss Mary died in January 1945 at the early age of fifty-six. She had been a mainstay – latterly the mainstay – of the school since she started teaching at the age of twenty-four having just left the Royal College of Music, back in the heroic age of Lloran House. Music was the centre of her life but she also taught divinity and history, sustained always by her deeply rooted Christian faith, a faith shown and given to all with whom she had contact. To quote from her obituary, 'Graciousness was the one quality, which perhaps more than any other, gave her a special place in the minds of her friends. No one who ever met her or was taught by her could fail to be impressed by her unfailing love of what was beautiful and worthwhile'.

It was wholly fitting that the memorial to Mary Lloyd-Williams and her mother ('Aunt Lil') should take the form of a sculpture, cast in bronze, depicting the heads of three girls, then members of the school, each playing an instrument – piano, violin and cello. The sculptor was Dr Karel Vogel and it stands appropriately by the school front door.

Bronwen Lloyd-Williams always said that she had no desire to be Principal of Moreton Hall. Nevertheless she felt the call of duty when her elder sister died. The school was flourishing but there was much to be done. In the war years expediency had seen the school through but now more long-term plans had to be made. Bronwen extricated herself from her London commitments with some difficulty and much was owed to Marion Halton Davis who frequently was called on to hold the fort at Moreton. Despite rationing and building restrictions the old barn was converted into accommodation in 1947 and the same year two substantial huts (with fireplaces) were acquired. In 1950 a much needed dining hall and modern kitchens were completed. The girls meanwhile picked up stones – as it seemed indefinitely – to make possible new playing fields.

But this improvement in the physical environment, important indeed, was nothing to the impact that Bronwen's permanent presence made on the whole school and all within it. Previously girls had known her as a ball of fire which erupted on Saturdays. Now in her long swinging skirts and long swinging earrings she seemed to be present all over the school, directing and energising others; and these post-war years were in some ways worse than the war years themselves with ever tighter rationing. How welcome was a gift, noted in the magazine, of 450lb of pearl barley and 150lb of oatmeal from Mrs Morris Eyton; and of a quantity of crockery from Mr Malkin.

In 1946 Bronwen produced a remarkable piece of choreography entitled World Crisis. The events preceding the war, the rise of the Axis powers, the war itself and its outcome, the aftermath of war and its suffering and the emergence of peace were the subjects, all danced to the music of The Planets by Holst. The finale showed the nations combining together to tackle the problems still to be faced such as the use of atomic energy. Apart from its artistic success – it was a real tour-de-force – the ballet showed Bronwen's

TRIO – Sculpture by Karel Vogel (Czechoslovakia).
Anne Stoner (Mrs Sawdy), Denise Bates (Mrs Rylands), Penelope Roles (Mrs Hersey).
Hand on violin Edith Edwards. Hand on violoncello Carl Fuchs.

Sunday best in the 1950s.

'Mamselle' Marie Le Caer and a group of foreign students.

deeply held personal belief in the importance of international relationship, when so many hopes in the post-war years were placed in the United Nations and other similar institutions before the Iron Curtain became a brutal check to optimists seeking a new era of peace.

International understanding became a central theme in the school, particularly membership and support for the Council of Education in World Citizenship which brought Miss L. E. Charlesworth, its Vice-Chairman and also Chairman of the Committee of the Association of Headmistresses, into close contact with Moreton. There were exchanges and visits to other countries and an increasing number of foreign girls came to the school. In 1950 there were two Greeks, one Persian, two Ethiopians, two French and two Dutch. Bronwen also appointed members of the staff from other countries. An impressive line up in 1949 included Mme Blondel of the Sorbonne, Mrs Singer Blau (who taught economics and World Citizenship), a student teacher Mme Monique Bouchend d'homme and Dr Risolo of the University of Florence. Perhaps it is an unworthy thought but this splendid roll call of names did not always reflect teaching ability in the classroom. Dr Risolo only lasted one term.

Bronwen herself attended conferences in Prague and in Paris and in 1951 was invited to spend three months in the USA at the invitation of the State Department to study an oddly assorted trio of subjects – education, medical rehabilitation and industry. Marion Halton Davis acted for her – her final contribution to the school which she had served so well.

There was a continual stream of distinguished visitors to the school: about this time came Sir Hartley Shawcross, the Attorney General; Professor Lancelot Hogben and Miss Winifred Cullis, both well known at the time; H. C. Dent, editor of the Times Educational Supplement; and the occasional Member of

1950. Miss Edwards conducts.

Miss Halton Davis.

Parliament. There was a constant programme of visits to concerts and events at other schools and a formidable list of lectures at Moreton, often on an international theme though one may wonder whether 'Industrial Health, Safety and Welfare in America' would keep the girls on the edge of their chairs. But that same term there were speakers on India, Canada, Indo-China, Russia and Malaya. United Nations week saw a packed programme of exhibitions, talks and drama with wonderfully colourful costumes. Lessons at prayers were read in different languages. Each form presented an episode from a different country.

1950s Staff Photograph

(Seated front left to right):
Miss Joan Pennington (now Mrs Franklin), Miss Dorothy Smith, Miss Edith Edwards, Miss Megan Thomas, Mademoiselle Marie Le Caer, Mrs Evelyn Richards, Miss Alice Halton Davis, Miss Rosalie Inskip.
(Behind right to left are included, some unidentified):
Miss Kitty Neligan (now Mrs Bill), Miss Doreen Cameron, Miss Priscilla Hoskyn, Miss Ursula Green, Miss Ruth Hannam, Senorita Maria Antonia Quiroga, Miss Davies (assistant matron – know as 'little Miss Davies'), Mrs Joan Marchant, Miss Ursula Roberts, Matron Edna Pooley, Miss Joy Moorhead.

III Bronwen – The Foundations

In 1950 there were 130 girls in the school and a staff of twenty-five. The new students' wing had now been opened. Mrs Richards was the Senior Mistress (she was nicknamed 'Osmosis' at this time because she used the word so frequently), Miss Cameron was Senior Housemistress and Miss Edwards was Bursar. Bronwen was now gathering about her what might in military parlance be called her General Staff. When she had taken over she had brought with her a person who was to play a central part for very many years – Joan Pennington. Only eighteen when she arrived and therefore much the same age as the senior girls, she became school Secretary and soon, with her total efficiency and dedication, became the central figure of the school administration, linked to every activity and a tower of strength to the many who consulted her. In 1948 Ursula Roberts, an Old Moretonian resident in Oswestry, joined the staff, nominally to assist in the office and act as receptionist. In her quiet way she soon expanded these roles to do many diverse things which no one else ever quite got round to doing. She became Librarian; and also treasurer of the Old Moretonians' Association. In 1952 Bronwen made an appointment of major significance when she brought Janet Norton to the school. Janet had – like Bronwen – been at the Bedford School of Physical Training and she brought with her many talents which matched those of Bronwen: she was a dancer and athlete of distinction, she played lacrosse at the highest level and she was a brilliant choreographer: she taught biology. In Joan, Janet and Ursula, Bronwen had an able General Staff and, it must be said, a team of ADCs who worked in the school until their respective retirements. It should be mentioned that Bronwen had also another team around her – the corgis whose life stories, ailments and replacements always had a paragraph in the Moretonian. Certain girls were dog monitoresses with defined corgi responsibilities.

Mrs Richards botanising.

1952. Mr Roberts, the cricketing Parson.

In 1951 and 1953 there were two outstanding dramatic productions which arose from Bronwen's friendship with Cyril Peckett, headmaster of the Priory Boys Grammar School in Shrewsbury. He was a man after her own heart being a classicist, a musician and a skilled director of plays. He was married to Mitzi Lawton who had been a professional pianist. Orpheus and Eurydice was a joint outdoor production of Moreton and the Priory at Shrewsbury Castle at which Cyril Peckett deployed his impressive choir of 150 boys. Even more ambitious was Dido and Aeneas, a floodlit production at Attingham Park with professional soloists: Heddle Nash sang Aeneas. Janet Norton and Doreen Cameron provided the ballet, most beautifully costumed. Attingham was then an Adult Education Centre run by the charismatic and gifted George Trevelyan who became an admirer and friend of Moreton to which he sent his daughter. Another interesting friend was Martin Wilson, the dynamic Director of Education for Shropshire, who – in alliance with Sir Offley Wakeman, Chairman of the County Council – propelled Shropshire to the very forefront of educational progress following the way pointed by the Butler 1944 Education Act.

In 1953 the fortieth anniversary was celebrated in due style. The gift of Old Moretonians was a desk and lectern carved in oak. Bronwen, generous as ever, gave a Bible and prayer book, beautifully bound in crimson leather and Dr Salt, another generous benefactor, gave the carpet, cushions and velvet fittings. At Parents' Weekend much of the school was decorated with posters and artistic variations on the school badge, made by Doreen Cameron's art students. There were performances of The Alchemist one of several productions by Joan Marchant, whose English teaching and play production was a feature of these years. The speaker was Mr Ivan Smith, a director of the United Nations Association.

It was Bronwen's idea that the blank walls in the new dining hall should be decorated with murals. Accordingly she commissioned Denise Bates, an Old Moretonian, to think of a theme and carry out the work. Denise was influenced by Rex Whistler and his murals which are still to be seen in the Tate restaurant. It was Denise's idea that the murals should indicate proverbs and she gradually carried out the work, taking time off to paint murals for a new Cunard liner and also to get married and become Mrs Rylands. The Moretonian reported that the murals were 'an

Dr Charles Salt, School Doctor for 40 years.

Miss Inskip

example of carefully planned composition, sure drawings and beautiful colour, with sufficient mystery in the delightful landscape to satisfy the most romantic, made highly entertaining and full in detail and finish'.

One of Bronwen's aims was to develop the Sixth Form. Whereas most girls in the past had taken the School Certificate, few had gone on to the Higher Certificate. In the 1950s the nomenclature of these exams changed to Ordinary Level and Advanced Level of the General Certificate of Education. In 1952 thirty-two girls took the 'O' level examination but only eight had five or more passes. Eleven took the 'A' level which was roughly the normal number, but only three passed in three or more subjects. Moreton did not show well as an academic school. Only one or two girls got to Oxford or Cambridge. It could of course be argued that women's academic qualities were not so regarded as today. The school was still very backward in science teaching and the whole curriculum was heavily weighted to the arts subjects. Bronwen aimed to build up the Sixth Form in both quantity and quality. The Student House helped in this; and the old dining hall became a library to which there were many gifts, not least from Bronwen herself. The old laundry was turned into a science laboratory. Thus it was hoped that academic standards would improve.

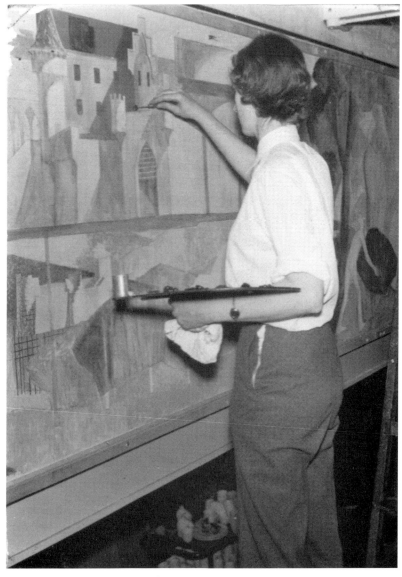

1954-55, Old Moretonian Mrs Denise Rylands busily painting the murals for the Dining Hall.

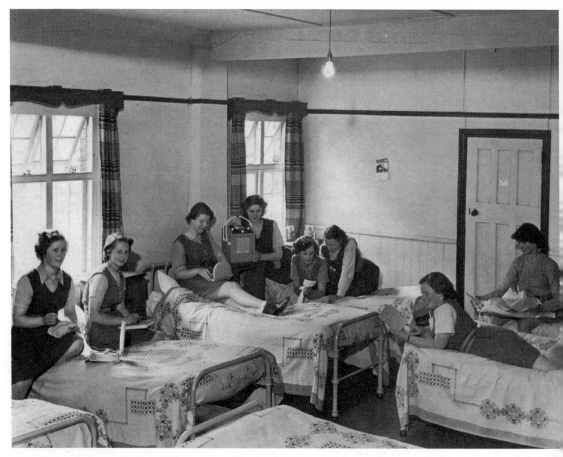

A dormitory in the 1950s.

Two activities which were inherent in the history of Moreton continued to flourish, girls were very successful in various public speaking competitions including the verse speaking contests run by the Shropshire Branch of the Classical Association. Elocution was, as always, given considerable emphasis.

From the earliest days there had been expeditions into the countryside and many elaborate picnics. One Old Moretonian remembers coming down Snowdon on the pig track, the girls singing 'Blest Pair of Sirens' in two-part harmony. Now more serious expeditions were undertaken and a Mountaineering Club established under the leadership of a new member of staff, Miss Green, herself trained in an Outward Bound School. Not only were the Welsh mountains tackled but in 1954 there was an expedition to the Norwegian mountains.

The outstanding event of 1955 was the opening of the outdoor theatre which had been two years in construction – a gift from Old Moretonians. Charles Morgan, the author and dramatic critic, performed the opening ceremony at Parents Weekend. 'Please go forward,' he said, 'with confidence in this adventure and if you are ever in doubt about too much solemnity or lightness of heart, choose the lightness of heart. Let your verse sing, let your step be lively, let your eyes shine and do not be afraid of extravagance.' It could certainly be said that the school and its Principal lived up to these words. The first performance was Thea Musgrave's ballet, A Tale of Thieves based on Chaucer's Pardoner's Tale, the music played by the composer and Rosalie Inskip with choreography by Janet Norton who played the principal part, and dressed by Doreen Cameron. This performance was followed by

1955. Miss Campbell, Miss Inskip and Miss Edwards.

1955. Paradise Lost. Mrs Marchant rehearses Pat Fender, Thea Musgrave and Elizabeth Brameld.

Paradise Lost, dramatised and produced by Joan Marchant, the two main roles being taken by Old Moretonians who were both professional actresses, Elizabeth Brameld and Pat Fender. Edith Edwards conducted the large choir and orchestra. Charles Morgan was generous in his praise: 'Pat Fender, as Adam, scores with grace and authority and Elizabeth Brameld's Satan is really outstanding, beautifully spoken and of rare distinction. But above all the collective performance holds its audience in that intense silence and stillness which the theatre always looks for and seldom attains.'

Pat Fender, who left Moreton in 1948, had had an outstanding school career culminating in being chosen as one of six students from Britain to take part in a Forum for High Schools in New York, organised by the Herald Tribune. She was the daughter of P. G. H. Fender, the England cricketer and captain of Surrey. He appeared in three Fathers' Matches in one of which he followed the precedent of W. G. Grace who, being bowled first ball, insisted on going on to bat, remarking to the bowler 'they have come to see me bat not you bowl'. Pat Fender later joined the staff for a period and became a professional actress. Later still, as Mrs Bensted-Smith, she sent her daughter to Moreton and was a Governor for some years. She also served a term as Secretary of the Old Moretonian Association.

1955. TALE FOR THIEVES. Thea Musgrave, MUS.BAC. (Mrs Mark).

1946 Tennis Team. Seated left: Pat Fender. Centre left: Denise Bates.

In the late 1950s numbers in the school continued to rise. There was an extension to the students' block and the old barn became the Fiction Library. The Sixth Form now numbered more than forty and the Transitional Form of girls between nine and eleven flourished. A sad loss was the death of Matron Pooley who had been in the school for many years. Wearing her Norland Nurse's uniform she was always visibly around the school, a neat little figure in brown. She was really Nanny to the whole community and a friend to all. Every Christmas she produced the nativity play with the junior girls which, in its sincerity, seemed to shed a spiritual radiance. When off duty, she went with her wheelbarrow to do a little planting or weeding.

Another who had become a great friend of the school was the Reverend A. C. Roberts, who retired from being school chaplain after many years' service which also extended to cricket coaching. Another much missed was Mr

Broughall, the school carpenter since – unbelievably – 1919. A skilled craftsman, there was practically no piece of furniture in the school which had not been touched by his hands. In 1935 he had constructed single handed the games pavilion; his last work was in the outdoor theatre. He was a man of stature in Weston Rhyn, an Elder of his Church and Sunday School Superintendent.

In 1960 there was an outstanding dramatic production entitled In My End is My Beginning – a pageant and indeed a spectacle which involved the whole school. The general theme was of teenagers facing the world in all its complexity, the war and its aftermath, the hopes of international co-operation, the contributions of children from various countries, the contrast of poverty and riches, the aspirations and work of the Council for Education in World Citizenship. The script was put together by Joan Marchant with imaginative

The open air theatre.

insight and most of the Moreton staff were involved; there was singing with the boys of the Priory School and members of the Oswestry Choral Society, dancing with choreography by Janet Norton and narration by Pat Salt and Elizabeth Brameld. The whole production was later taken to Wandsworth School for a massive performance with members of sixteen schools, directed in the final and only full rehearsal by Bronwen herself, armed with her whistle from lacrosse days. The Queen sent a telegram and various representatives of international bodies attended led by Miss L. E. Charlesworth, a close friend to Moreton, Chairman of C.E.W.C.

Lower School singing.

Moreton Hall School from the air, 1956.

IV BRONWEN – FULFILMENT

In 1963 Bronwen had been Principal for eighteen years. She had become one of the outstanding Headmistresses of the day; and there were ten more years to come. Wherein did her strengths lie? Many would say in the depth of her understanding of each of her pupils, to be valued and loved as unique individuals. She believed passionately in what were in the Sixties regarded as old fashioned virtues – consideration for others, good manners, self-discipline and courage. But her view of the world was anything but old-fashioned for she consciously set about training Moretonians in world citizenship and to have some understanding of how society worked and of international affairs. Hence the number of girls from different countries who came to the school, the development of links and activities with the Council for Education in World Citizenship, the United Nations Association and the English Speaking Union, through which machinery girls were constantly selected to cross the Atlantic for seminars or attachments. Distinguished guests always seemed to be arriving for some function or other – a Nigerian Cabinet Minister, a University Professor, a Bishop, a member of one of the Embassies, a Member of Parliament, the Prime Minister of Northern Ireland.

Every year the school calendar charted a wide ranging series of lectures, of concerts, of visits and of expeditions. The school might be deep in the country but every endeavour was made to keep the girls in touch with the wider world. Within the school the standard of music and of drama and dance was a constant surprise to visitors. Bronwen was fortunate to have so talented team – Edith Edwards (until her sad death in 1961) and Rosalie Inskip, both outstanding musicians, Janet Norton's arrangements of ballet and dance, Joan Marchant's skill in the adaptation (where necessary) and production of classic plays and always unobtrusively at hand Doreen Cameron's splendid costumes.

STANISLAV AND ELISAVETA
Stanislav (K. Casewell)   Elisaveta (M. Davey)
Snobbery (V. Prosser)   Red Tape (A. Prowse)

Co-operation with boys' schools was developed in the 1960s and there would be parties and dances at Lindisfarne College, at Shrewsbury School – and some cricket and tennis at Oswestry School and Ellesmere. When Richard Sale was newly arrived as Headmaster of Oswestry, it was Bronwen who organised a welcoming party presided over by Jack Peterson, Headmaster of Shrewsbury. Cultural co-operation was more difficult owing to the distances involved though there were joint General Studies classes with Ellesmere for some time and, of course, boys came and sang in the Moreton concerts.

Ian Beer in his memoirs (But Headmaster! Greenbank Press) writes of attending a ball at Moreton with thirty Sixth Formers, he being the newly appointed Headmaster of Ellesmere:

> When we arrived all our pupils vanished on to the dance floor and I was taken on one side by Bronwen. To my horror she said 'Ian, come and have a gin with me in my study'. 'And what about Angela [his wife]?' I said. 'Oh there are a lot of delightful young men from other schools who will be delighted to dance with her'. Bronwen was clearly someone who was used to being obeyed. The gin in her study turned out to be more a bottle than a glass and, by the time I reached the dance floor, I was well away. Next day we wrote our thank you letters and I received a call from Bronwen asking me whether I had checked all the studies of my sixth formers to make certain each boy had received a red rose from one of her girls.

One characteristic of Bronwen was her capacity for being entirely down to earth. She liked to deal with matters briefly and with a touch of humour. When Martin Wilson, Director of Education for Shropshire, wrote with some concern about his daughter's academic progress, he received in reply an open postcard which read 'Received your letter. Don't fuss. Yours Bronwen.' For breaches of discipline she had her own methods of punishment, perhaps a passage from Shakespeare or Milton to be learned in the hours before breakfast and then written down with complete accuracy including the punctuation. Bronwen was a heavy smoker but came down heavily on girls caught smoking. To one she said 'So you like smoking. Here is a packet of ten. Go outside and smoke them and come back when you have finished.' Only a short time later the girl came back, green in face, not having made much impression on the packet which had made a considerable impression on her.

One wonders how OFSTED inspectors would react. Nor were her criteria for appointing staff in any way orthodox. A lady recently widowed with three children replied to an advertisement for an Assistant Matron. At the end of the interview Bronwen said 'I don't want you as a Matron. But I've got a class who are rather awkward at the moment, the Transitional, and I'm fed up with graduates who don't understand children. You're a mother so you'll understand them so you're appointed as a teacher.' The applicant staggered out of the room in a state of shock. She had left school at sixteen and had no qualifications whatsoever.

To her pupils her advice was always direct and definite. At the beginning of term she would say, 'Write a proper letter to your parents thanking them for

Anyone for tennis?

Bronwen and the Corgis.

the holidays; don't send them a scruffy postcard asking for your toothbrush.' She was not tolerant of minor irritants: 'Stop coughing. You can if you try.' She was also capable of grand gestures. After many had suffered from 'flu, she cancelled all normal activity for the day and sent the whole school off to the Welsh hills to breathe the fresh air. When dealing with prospective parents (in the trade sense) her psychology was to concentrate on the father. While mother was sent off to look around the bedrooms, father was taken for a walk in the rose garden. By the time the mother appeared they were well into the gin. Brothers too, were welcomed. If a boy behaved well he could expect to have a ten shilling note in his hand to go home with. Boys in the mass, however, were looked at with suspicion. When Moreton played Ellesmere at tennis (at home) the school were not allowed to watch lest passions be aroused. Fathers of Head Prefects had to pay the penalty of making a speech at Parents' Weekend, causing waves of anxiety in the family weeks ahead. Bronwen loved these state occasions which she carried off in style, always appearing in a new hat often of astonishing proportions.

By the 1960s she had built up the Sixth Form to between sixty and seventy. But Moreton could still not be recognised as an academic school. Every year six or seven girls went to universities including one or two to Oxford or Cambridge, but only about the same number achieved three A levels. Those not going to universities went to training colleges, hospital schools, colleges of domestic science, schools of art and nursery training.

Another aspect of Bronwen was her personal generosity to the school. When a new library was set up she gave the shelves, which were of the highest quality; when the dress of the choir for religious services was under discussion she gave a complete set of cassocks; when the school purchased an epidiascope she gave the screen; when there were trees to be planted, she gave them; and always an annual gift of books to the libraries.

Sir George Trevelyan was the principal guest at Parents' Weekend in 1962. He was the Warden of the Adult Education College at Attingham Park, which he ran with charismatic panache, and had been a good friend to Moreton over the years, bringing parties of visiting Americans to visit the school and

The Marchant Gallery before being rebuilt.

Bronwen in her prime.

welcoming girls to participate in the wide ranging courses and conferences which he ran. His daughter was Head Prefect so Sir George found himself having to speak for the parents. This is part of his address:

> Something happens to your daughters when they go to Moreton. From the first touch with the spirit of the place they begin to show poise, a pride of bearing, an outgoing and friendly touch with people and a social confidence to meet the world without by any means losing their sense of fun. The school develops a full and balanced approach to life and its true beauties. It is no small thing that girls here can, as a natural thing, take part in great works like the Brahms Requiem and the Matthew Passion, that you can make and perform your own ballet, act Shakespeare, beat all comers at lacrosse, swing with the best and put exams in the place they should be, as hurdles to be taken in the stride. You show a seriousness of purpose without allowing yourselves to get too solemn. You are full of life and know that life is shot through with humour.

The founders of the school might well have been pleased to hear this encomium which so well summed up all their hopes of fifty years ago.

Moreton Hall was the personal property of Bronwen Lloyd-Williams. In 1962 in order to ensure the future she decided to set up an Educational Trust whose members, the Trustees, would own the school. In doing this she was following the trend of those days when proprietary schools were rapidly diminishing in number. Apart from other considerations the death duties on the death of a proprietor would be a heavy burden. As Chairman of the new Governing Body, Bronwen invited Major A. H. Gem. Bronwen had got to know him through her membership of the committee of the Central Council for Physical Recreation, for her enthusiasm for the encouragement of physical activity continued from her own active days. Arthur Gem, a solid and sensible retired soldier, was the Vice-Chairman of the C.C.P.R. What kindled Bronwen's enthusiasm even more for this body was the fact that the Duke of Edinburgh was the President. It was remarkable how often Prince Philip crept into Bronwen's conversation at this time.

An old friend from London, Dr M. A. Adams became (temporarily) Vice-Chairman of the Governors. Other members were: Alderman S. G. D. Campbell of Oswestry; Miss L. E. Charlesworth, former President of the Association of Headmistresses; the Hon. V. H. O. Herbert, Director of Shelton Iron and Steel Company; Dr J. Marchant; B. L. Pearson, former Accountant General to the Minister of Education; C. H. Wallace Pugh, solicitor in Oswestry; R. Sale, Headmaster of Oswestry School; Martin Wilson, Secretary of the Shropshire Local Education Authority; and two Old Moretonians, Mrs Denise Rylands and Mrs Margaret Williams. J. L. Knight was the accountant and auditor to the Trust and J. I. Williams its solicitor. The Trust operated from 1st January 1964.

The value of the school was assessed at £80,000, this sum to be paid to Bronwen by debentures over sixteen years; her personal living costs were to be paid by the Trust and, after retirement, £1000 per annum.

V BRONWEN – APOTHEOSIS

Little was changed by the establishment of the Trust. Having surrounded herself with her friends as Governors, Bronwen continued to run the school for the next eight years in her own inimitable style. Several long time friends of the school died or retired at this time. Grace Lloyd-Williams died in 1964. She had retired in 1953 but had taken a leading part in establishing the school in its earliest days before the war. Dr Salt, school doctor for forty years, retired in 1960. Apart from his work as school doctor he had been a generous benefactor and involved himself closely in the running of the school. His place was taken by his son, Dr Pat Salt. His partner of many years, Dr Hampson, died in this same year; in the old days he had many times judged the gymkhana. Edith Edwards died in 1961. She had been in charge of the music since 1945 and had made a wonderful contribution in so many concerts, ballets and plays. She was equally loved by the Oswestry Choral Society which she had conducted for many years. In 1968 Mrs Richards' long Moreton career came to an end, teaching to the last days of her life, though latterly she came only to do part-time coaching. She had come to the school after the death of her distinguished husband, (the Richards of the Morley-Richards firm). She had first class degrees in chemistry and botany and scholarships in history and economics – she was in fact a polymath and certainly the most academically distinguished teacher at Moreton in her time. Many Moretonians, now doctors and scientists, owe her much. She was splendidly eccentric and highly regarded by all.

Others came to take the place of those who had gone. The language teaching developed in the hands of Aine Moore, Head of Staff; and of Bruna Hodges, an excellent German teacher. Henry Maas headed the classical teaching and wrote a book on the letters of Ernest Dowson which gave Bronwen the excuse of holding a launch party. At this time Judy Roe and

50th birthday celebrations.

1964. Bronwen Lloyd-Williams with Parents' Weekend guests and Dr Pat Salt.

Merriel Halsall-Williams started their long connection with the school. Academic results were improving and, for instance, thirteen girls went to universities in 1967. Every year prizes and awards were won at the Chester Festival of Speech and Drama, at the Royal Academy of Dancing and Ballet, the English Speaking Board and Classical Speaking Board; there was always an impressive list of those taking the Associated Board examinations in music in the various grades.

The Governors were much exercised at this time by the problem of the school finances at a time of mounting inflation – a problem which was to be with them for a number of years. The basic salaries of the staff were tied to the Burnham Scale which was paid to teachers in the state system. The scale was constantly being raised as a result of various reports, by figures as high as ten or fifteen per cent. What was most difficult for the school was that the awards were generally retrospective by as much as five months; yet the fees charged to parents, which were Moreton's only income, could not be raised retrospectively. So it was a question of timing – to raise the fees sufficiently to pay the new salaries and in retrospect – what one might guess that Burnham would be. There was also a natural hesitancy in raising the fees, even when sufficient warning was given, and in retrospect the Governors should have been bolder in raising fees higher and sooner. It is easy to say after the event and many independent schools made the same mistake. On one occasion cash flow simply did not enable the retrospective element to be paid at once and the staff had to wait for their increase which caused grumbling from some few. To build the science building, for the first time the Governors took out a loan of £35,000 from the Midland Bank secured by a mortgage on the Trust's freehold property. This loan of course had to be serviced annually.

In 1972 there was, for the first time, a revenue deficit; although the revenue had increased by five per cent expenses had increase by elevern per cent. The school accountant put the matter bleakly: either expenses must be reduced or the numbers in the school increased or the fees must go up to unprecedented height.

Speech Day, 1967. Guests of Honour: Dr J. Karefa-Smart, Assistant Director General, World Health Organisation, and his wife. They presented a trophy which is annually awarded.

Another matter which worried the Governors – as in all independent schools – was the general attack by the Labour Government of Harold Wilson. In view of much hostility, the time honoured devise of appointing a Royal Commission was put into play. The school had to provide a mass of information both to the Commission and also to the Governing Body of Girls' Schools Association which, together with the Headmasters Conference and other bodies, were fighting the radical proposals which were being floated. It did indeed seem possible that independent education would become illegal. In the event the Commission's Report in 1968 was wholly ignored by the Government. Its main proposal was that, over a period of years, fifty per cent of pupils at public schools should be composed of those with boarding need – another way of saying 'deprived'; an unashamed piece of social engineering. Noel Annan, a member of the Commission, later wrote 'of all the futile committees on which I have sat, none equalled the Public School Commission'.

The New Hall was erected in 1967; it came as a gift from the Orthopaedic Hospital at Gobowen. It lessened the pressure on the gymnasium and gave space for rehearsals of choir, orchestra or drama. The major event of 1968 was the opening of the science block at Parents' Weekend, a badly needed addition to the Moreton facilities. The opening was by Dr John Hawksley of University College London; he was accompanied by his wife Dr Margaret Hawksley and the building was blessed by the Bishop of Birmingham, the Right Reverend J. L. Wilson. Despite a heavy storm, the weekend was a great success and the evening entertainment was a ballet to the music of Beethoven's Eighth Symphony, arranged by Janet Norton, and a performance of Joan Marchant's adaptation of Paradise Lost. Four years later the new music block was opened by one of the most charming visitors ever to come to Moreton – Lady Barbirolli. There was a programme of musical activities by the girls and a Recital by Lady Barbirolli (her professional name was Evelyn Rothwell) on the oboe accompanied by Rosalie Inskip. Lady Barbirolli was Professor of Oboe at the Royal Academy of Music.

For many years all the building and maintenance work had been directed by Mr F. G. Salway F.R.I.C.S. and the school owed much to his capacity for both the planning and execution of the work in connection with the science and music buildings. Being a local man he was knowledgeable about contractors and sub-contractors and he also directed the school's small but skilled workforce who loyally served Moreton over many years.

As might be expected the fiftieth anniversary of the founding of the United Nations Organisation was vigorously celebrated. A two day conference was held to which came sixth formers from eight Shropshire schools. There was an address by Miss L. E. Charlesworth on what proved to be her last visit to the

Annabel Hunt, Mary King, Lady Barbirolli, Sarah Reid, Mary Giffard.

school, a study of the place of Israel, a discourse on America in the Sixties and discussion groups on a variety of subjects, the course culminating in a Brains Trust with the headmaster of Ellesmere, David Skipper, in the chair.

Bronwen was untiring in her enthusiasm for the understanding of other cultures and continued to welcome foreign girls to Moreton, in whom she often had a deep pastoral interest. Being in loco parentis to Princess Mahrsende of Ethiopia, she was influential in arranging her marriage to Prince Sahle Selassie, son of the Emperor. Bronwen met the Emperor once but was unable to persuade him to visit the school At another time an Iranian pupil was short listed to be the wife of the Shah. She was a high profile girl as her mother was the wife of Iskander Mirza, President of Pakistan. Bronwen defused press speculation and interference by hiding the girl away in her Cardiganshire house, much enjoying these skirmishes with reporters, harking back to her own time as a journalist.

Numbers in the school kept up well in the 1960s rising to 260 in 1969. This was remarkable in that this was the time when boys' public schools were opening their Sixth Forms to girls and when Sixth Form colleges were being established. A number of girls did leave to pursue their Sixth Form studies elsewhere but it was not difficult to find Sixth Form entrants to Moreton. More intangible and more difficult to deal with were the wishes of senior girls for more privileges and more freedom in line with the general relaxation of society in that decade of student unrest. Bronwen steered with a firm hand but made a number of small changes and modifications even going to the length of allowing girls who were addicted to tobacco to smoke an evening

1968 Parents' Weekend. Dr John Hawksley, Bronwen Lloyd-Williams, Major Gem, Mrs Hawksley, the Bishop of Birmingham.

cigarette with her in the drawing room with parents' consent. She always said she had no difficulty recruiting staff and seldom had to advertise. In retrospect it might perhaps be thought that not all the new recruits were of the highest quality. There was certainly a lack of quality in the 'A' level results; in 1968 there was a total of only six A grades papers amongst thirty-one candidates. The familiar statement that girls don't do science was certainly borne out at Moreton. In 1969, a typical year, there was only one pass in chemistry, two in physics and four in zoology.

Bronwen was good at attracting well known people not only to come and visit and speak but to send their daughters. It did the school no harm to have, at different times, the granddaughters of Bertrand Russell, the daughter of Richard Hughes, the author, and of the Prime Minister of Northern Ireland; and the daughter of Frederick Gibberd, the architect of the Catholic cathedral in Liverpool (who took a conducted party of girls round the building), of the Bishop of Chester and of the Headmaster of Shrewsbury School.

Various events stand out in the Sixties. Most unusual was the Beating of Retreat by the Band and Bugles of the 2nd Gurkhas, together with their Pipes and Drums, the tough fighting men from the Himalayas merging incongruously into the peaceful Shropshire landscape. In 1964 there was a visit to Russia by a school party, led by Baron von der Pahlen, who taught Russian and was one of Bronwen's more exotic appointments. Having escaped the 1917 Revolution, he was brought up in Germany, then went to Oxford and was interned in 1940. On release he essayed to travel to Canada but his ship was torpedoed. Rescued from the water he went to Australia for the war years before returning to England. His uncle was the Patriarch of the Russian Orthodox Church whom the Moreton girls met in Moscow. The girls were convinced that the Baron was a spy!

There was also an Educational Cruise to East Africa at this time and in 1971 the 2500th anniversary of the Persian Royal Family was celebrated with an elaborate dinner for the eight Persian girls in the school. A telegram was sent to the Shah who graciously replied. (But the days of his regime were numbered.) The same year there was an outstanding school production. The Vision of Atlantis written by Jill Lawson who was on the history staff. The play was an elaborate allegory, based on the legends of the lost continents of Atlantis and Lemuria, which are said to lie beneath the Atlantic and the Pacific oceans respectively. This was one of the last productions of Joan Marchant, with accompanying ballet arranged by Janet Norton and dressed by Doreen Campbell. In another sphere of activities the school won the Benenden Cup, for the second year running, the All England Schools lacrosse championship.

In 1970 the Governing Council was weakened by the sad death of one of its most active members, Miss L. E. Charlesworth, a close friend of the school over many years and also the representative of Moreton on the Governing Bodies of Girls' Schools Association. At this time three new Governors were appointed – Pat Fender, Kenneth Todd, a recently retired Inspector of Education, and Michael Charlesworth, lately Principal of Lawrence College, Pakistan, and now Second Master at Shrewsbury School. Shortly after this John Knight took over from his father as Accountant to the Governors.

In 1971 at the request of Old Moretonians, a portrait of Bronwen was painted by Denise Bates (Mrs Rylands) which hangs in the Hall. The comments of the subject are pertinent and typical:

> Had I refused the very kind and well-intentioned request from Old Moretonians it would have been churlish and ungrateful; no one could have been more considerate than Denise Rylands, who carried out the formidable task with infinite patience, tolerance and skill. It is excellently painted, and, regrettably, just like me; so there instead of 'hanging as high Haman' I hang in Moreton and dare not put under the painting the title Portrait of a Welsh Witch, which, in my opinion, would be a very apt description for, alas, I was born at midnight on All Hallows E'en, although I strive to claim the 1st November as my birthday, in company with the Saints!

Bronwen's general summing up of the state of the school at this time is expressed at the conclusion of her Report to the Governors in 1972:

> Where the Governors are concerned, I can only say that without their help and support, we should not be where we are. As it is we are a very fortunate community, beset occasionally by doubt, dangers and fears of possible disasters, always rectified in time by team-work, optimism and scholarly ability. All – school, staff, Governors and and Guiding Spirits – work to one end, putting up with my personal idiosyncrasies and flights of fancy, trimming the ship where necessary, piloting it towards success in such a way that it is once more an understatement to say that their combined efforts produce what is little short of miraculous.

Somewhat overblown as this wordy statement might be, the reference to 'idiosyncrasies' would certainly be echoed by Chairman Arthur Gem who described the Principal in an unguarded aside as an absolutely impossible woman!

VI REGIME CHANGE

Bronwen was now in her seventieth year. She had been in her usual form as her Report to the Governors showed. 'The Matron's Department has been consuming much time and boredom.' 'As my staff knows, anything I take on involves a great deal of work for others.' When plays in Greek and German were performed she was aware that 'it puts a considerable tax on parents'. She continued to direct in her own inimitable manner. Girls deemed unsuitable were sent on their way; staff who did not come up to her standards were propelled elsewhere, arising from which solicitors sometimes had work to do. Occasional collisions there certainly were but Bronwen continued to ride the waves with total self-confidence. However in the autumn of 1970 she showed for the first time that she was not immortal and intimated to her Governors that the time would come when she would retire and they should be forewarned in order to take steps which they thought appropriate which she would not in the least resent.

In the summer of 1971 Bronwen had a serious operation and was absent for both the summer and winter terms but was back in the saddle at the beginning of 1972, for the opening of the music building and the usual activities, appointing seven new members of staff and coping with the fact that one Matron had a baby on the Sunday of Parents' Weekend. Looking ahead she, for the first time, agreed in principle to the launching of an Appeal, something which she had hitherto opposed. The Principal's Report to the Governors for the period to October 1972 was the last to bear the signature of Bronwen Lloyd-Williams.

She had a bad dose of 'flu in the autumn of 1972, partly brought on by her insistence on going to London to a function where Prince Philip was present. That Christmas she spent alone in her flat in London and returned to Moreton with intense depression, increased by the news of the death of her sister Kitty. She was clearly very ill but it took the combined efforts of her doctor and several friends to persuade her to go into hospital in London. She recognised that the time had come. She wrote out her resignation to the Governors.

At a meeting in March 1973, the Governors faced the key question – whether to advertise the post of Principal or to appoint Janet Norton who had been Vice-Principal for fifteen years, and who had successfully run the school in Bronwen's absence with the powerful support of Joan Pennington. It was decided by a single vote to advertise and the General Purposes Committee, recently invented, was asked to draw up the terms and conditions for the advertisement. But at the next Governors' meeting, a fortnight later, a Governor who had not been at the former meeting now being present, the Chairman managed to reverse the previous decision and Janet Norton was appointed Principal with immediate effect.

The decision was made by the narrowest of margins and it is perhaps worth noting that those Governors who were, or had been, professionally engaged in education all voted in the minority. Those in favour of the appointment of Janet Norton argued that it was essential to end what had been quite a long period of uncertainty, that Janet Norton had been successfully running the school for the last year or more; that Bronwen had always assumed that Janet would succeed her and, on a material point, where was the salary of an outside Principal to come from? Those who were in favour of advertising argued that it was essential to choose from as wide a field as possible and that Janet Norton could apply if she so wished; her position would be strengthened, if appointed, in that she had faced competition; her lack of academic qualifications would handicap the school in the academic field.

All the Governors without exception appreciated and admired the work she had done in the school over many years. But those who had doubts could see that someone who was an admirable number two would not necessarily make number one; and those who knew her well also knew that she had no wish to become Principal and would take it on as a duty rather than look on the post as an exciting opportunity. However the die was cast and Janet became Principal, from the beginning of the Summer Term 1973. The situation was complicated in that Bronwen showed no inclination to move out of her flat, though tentative steps were taken to find a house in Chirk. She certainly intended to stay for the Summer Term and indeed at one time advanced the suggestion that she should stay indefinitely on the analogy of Lady Berwick, who lived on at Attingham, though the house and estate were owned and run by the National Trust. For the new Principal in her first term what should have been a bright prospect was considerably muddied over in having to cope with the presence of her predecessor ensconced in the very heart of the school. However the situation was suddenly and tragically transformed: Bronwen took her own life and was found dead in her bedroom.

So, sadly, ended twenty-eight years of remarkable and charismatic leadership which had seen Moreton grow from a roll of one hundred to two hundred and fifty. The reader of the preceding pages will have comprehended the scale and manner of her achievement. The plaque which was erected outside the front door, opposite the memorial to her mother and sister, records 'her vision and courage which gave the school scholarship, gaiety and humanity'. A memorial service in the gymnasium was very fully attended, not only by Old Moretonians but by people from the district and from various bodies for which she worked. The Address was by her friend from the Council for World Citizenship, Terence Lawson, but he had little to say about the school, which was her life's work. He ended: 'It is said of some people that they are larger than life. It is the supreme triumph of Bron that she was larger than death.'

The readings and music covered her well loved authors – T. S. Eliot, Dylan Thomas, John Donne, Henry Vaughan and John Milton; and, of course, there was Sydney Carter's Lord of the Dance. Remarkably there was no obituary in the Moretonian.

Bronwen Lloyd-Williams had personified Moreton Hall and it was difficult to think of the school without her. Whoever succeeded, the task would be difficult. Janet Norton had the advantage of knowing the school intimately and being known by parents, staff and girls; there would be continuity – and she was loyally supported. Joan Pennington, who had a wide ranging grasp of the administration, was at her side, always prepared to work long hours and take responsibility when needed.

To the Governors, however, meeting after Bronwen's death, it soon became apparent what a law unto herself she had been. She and the Governors had been fortunate to be able to draw on the skills of Messrs. Williams, Knight and Salway skilled consultants in the realms of the law, accountancy and building and at this time of transition to a new regime their advice was badly needed. Hitherto Governors had been invited to join the Council by Bronwen, without any other formality. Now it was found that apart from the original members, none had signed the necessary Document of Consent as laid down by the Companies Act. More serious the Articles of Association (as drawn up by the Governing Bodies of Girls' Schools Association) had never been followed. There had been no Annual General Meetings, no election of Chairman and officers, no machinery for the election of new members or the retirement of existing ones, in fact, while nothing illegal had been done, the whole structure of the Council had been faulty. All this had to be put right. At the same time Joan Pennington was appointed Secretary to the Council. To improve the general machinery of government, a Finance and General Purpose Committee of five was set up.

Several new Governors were appointed at this time; one of the most useful was David Pilkington, a parent, who brought a wealth of experience from his work in his great family firm. The family connection was maintained through the appointment of Colonel J. A. Lloyd-Williams, a nephew of Bronwen's, and her sister Betty (Mrs Brett) became President of the Old Moretonians Association which had a very active life with meetings in the summer at Moreton and in the winter in London. The Secretary was Margaret Williams and the Treasurer Ursula Roberts; an examination of the magazines of this period show their industry and skill in keeping the Association going and in the maintenance of detailed records of Old Moretonians.

Before Bronwen's death it had been decided to launch an appeal with professional fund raisers and two objectives were chosen – the building of a Sixth Form boarding house (subsequently called the Lloyd-Williams House as a memorial to Bronwen) and a swimming pool. Colonel L. Young was the representative of Richard Maurice and Co. and went about his business in 1974 and 1975. The appeal had considerable success and by May 1974 £63,000 was given or promised though only £13,000 was in cash in the bank. Nonetheless the decision was taken to go ahead with the new House most of which was in use by the summer of 1975.

However in the year 1974 and 1975 the Governors faced a bleak financial outlook. It was perhaps inevitable that numbers would go down after Bronwen's death but the decline was steep. Whereas there had been 260 girls in 1969, there were 219 in 1975. Economies had to be employed in every field, none more than in the matter of staffing. Bronwen had had a somewhat cavalier attitude to the engagement of staff, filling vacancies (or creating new posts) as seemed appropriate. When Martin Wilson sought advice from a professional firm of educational consultants in London and revealed the staffing ratio eyebrows shot up and astonishment was expressed. Janet Norton did her best and managed to reduce the staff by four and a half posts during her time as Principal but, with inflation careering along, there was an overdraft of £45,000 in 1975. Bursaries were cut, music was to be charged for rather than included in the fee and an attempt – unsuccessful – was made to recruit day girls. Meanwhile the Government relentlessly increased teachers' salaries on the Burnham scale. In 1974 there was an especially large increase – the Houghton award, backdated by several months. The school simply could not pay this backdated element and the Chairman had so to inform the staff, promising to pay at a future date when circumstances allowed, pointing out that it was more important to keep the school going – and maintain their jobs – than to bankrupt it by this payment. There were complaints from some and the threat of action in the Courts. This proved to be one of the last actions of Arthur Gem – a distasteful one sadly – as he resigned as Chairman and member of the Governing Council in April 1975; his had been a solid and dependable presence over the previous decade, a counsellor in good times and bad, with a deep devotion to the school. He was succeeded as Chairman by Michael Charlesworth.

Away from the Boardroom and unworried by these concerns, the school continued to function normally. It is perhaps a time to take a look at the internal machinery by which daily life was conducted. For many years various duties and responsibilities had been discharged by the ten or so prefects, together with about the same number of sub-prefects. They worked through a number of committees, the composition of which resulted in considerable discussion. The Bounds committee saw to it that all girls understood the extremely complex directions as to where one might or might not go. For instance: Out of Bounds areas:

> Front stairs (except for prefects)
> Front door (except for Upper Sixth)
> Front garden (except for Sixth Forms)
> Front drive – no further than the bridge
> Back drive – no-one at all... etc. etc.
> Sunbathing was allowed in the outdoor theatre (Decently dressed – no
> swim suits) and in the games field – far corner only by the flower beds
> – swim suits allowed etc. (What did etc. mean?)

There was another rule which came under the Bounds committee – no running in the dark. There is constant reference to this rule being broken; presumably the culprits ran faster than the prefects?

There were committees to check tidiness in dormitories and tidiness in form rooms: to check the putting out of lights: to supervise the tuck shop and the potentially unruly queue which formed outside it: and to see that the TV room was kept in order. For infringements of all sorts there were penalties reckoned in Order Marks (10) Intermediate Marks (7) and Punctuality Marks (4). Totals were kept for each House (or Sett: there were now four with the addition of Marchant's) and running totals read out at morning assembly. The ultimate penalty was two hours' detention on Saturday evenings.

The working of all these committees and the problems which arose were discussed at Prefects' Meetings, with the Principal in the chair, held twice a term at which full minutes were kept. Reading these minutes covering a number of years the reader is both intrigued and bored as the same subjects come up again and again and again. Dress is a prime example – who could wear what and when.

> 'Anybody whose hair touches their collar or falls over their face must wear a hairband; grips are not sufficient.'
> 'No rings not even engagement rings to be worn.' (sic)
> 'In cold weather people must not take liberties by wearing woollen scarves, long boots, patterned or long black stocking.'
> 'All Sunday dresses 6½" above the knee. Coats 6". Djibbahs must cover pants.'
> 'Every day shoes should be no higher than two inches.'
> 'When the weather gets hotter it was decided that only socks need to be worn.' (Perhaps something was omitted here?)

The variations and possibilities of dress were a limitless matter for discussion.

Never ending debate centres round the dining hall – how to get 250 girls in and out of the hall without confusion; how to get food distributed to the tables each of which had a Table Head; and the quality of the food itself. It was true of course that the hall was too small for the number it contained so the noise level tended to be high. No prefects, meeting was complete without suggestions or complaints about the dining hall. When a formal meal with the staff was held in order to add a touch of dignity and encourage good table manners, the representative of the Fifth Form said that 'her form found it utmost difficult to eat slowly.' When the kitchen had to cope with a lunch for visitors, the girls' breakfast, eaten in form rooms, was a Mars Bar and bread; actually the variation was not unpleasing – and there were always buns in the break.

The telephone was another centre of dispute; it was laid down that certain forms could use it at certain hours, that some could receive incoming calls, that others could make outgoing calls. But the rules were always being questioned and complaints made about wrongful use. When grateful parents gave an iron and ironing board at once it became the centre of controversy as to who could use it and when.

It can be seen that the prefects had a big job to impose the boundaries laid down in various spheres. Bronwen had various directives for the prefects, often reiterated, the main one being that the example they set was the only way of earning respect. She emphasised that when out on leave they were to stay in threes and not to vary from the object and place of visit; they were not to drink spirits but a small quantity of wine was permissible: they were to behave quietly in public and never to discuss members of the staff adversely. They were not to arrange surreptitious meetings with young men; to go out with a young man, parental permission was required. There was to be no smoking and no driving of cars. On the subject of dress Bronwen said she expected them 'to be chic but not outré'.

When Bronwen was Principal she dealt firmly but sensitively with the desire of the prefects for change at a time when authority was being challenged in many fields, not least by school girls and boys. Her imperium was so complete that she could not really be challenged. Janet Norton's position was less strong. She was essentially conservative and reluctant to change the Moreton structure of life in which she had been central for twenty years. The continual niggling of the prefects, particularly in the matter of exeats and dress regulations she found difficult to deal with. There was constant pressure that the hours when the various age groups might have exeats, either with parents or to shop in Oswestry or elsewhere should be extended. In general, Janet resisted. As she said to one of her Governors, 'I have fought them every inch of the way' – which did not seem to indicate a happy relationship with those who should be her major supporters. She found much to criticise in the present generation, speaking of 'the terrible apathy within the school', complaining of untidiness of dress, warning against the use of bad language and also the dangers of gossip. She also had to cope with a less than positive attitude to church going – always one of the main pillars of the Moreton establishment.

Janet gave herself wholly to the school as she always had done and strove to carry out the duties of Principal. But she suffered from the stress and strain in filling a position to which she was not suited. She was entirely honest, though undiplomatic, in expressing her distaste. In March 1975, after one or two private consultations, she announced her intention to resign as soon as a successor could be appointed expressing the hope that she might be allowed to resume her position of Vice-Principal. Her resignation was accepted and not entirely unexpected; it was agreed that she should revert to being Vice-Principal.

Despite the aggravations referred to and Janet's criticisms, it would be wrong to suggest that life at Moreton in the three years when Janet was Principal in any way deteriorated. The normal activities were pursued, the traditions were upheld, Parents' Weekend took place in its summer glory though undecorated by Bronwen's hats. Fathers of different shapes turned out dutifully to play cricket against the school, mothers confronted their offspring across the tennis net. The father of the Head Prefect continued to be offered up as an annual tribal sacrifice and made his platform speech after his daughter had made hers.

There was drama and music in the Moreton tradition: a joint concert with Ellesmere College of Mendelssohn's Elijah: a dance interpretation of Beethoven's Eighth Symphony the production of the mediaeval morality play, Everyman. The school heard Rohan de Saram play the cello and James Blades his many percussion instruments. In fact it was not proving easy to maintain the school's musical reputation to match the standards of the Edith Edwards and Rosalie Inskip era, especially as fewer girls learned music after the imposition of charges for lessons. In 1973 there was a holiday expedition to Russia; and United Nations week was celebrated in what had become traditional form. A devastating 'flu epidemic hit the school in the winter of 1974, three-quarters of the girls being afflicted, the virulence of this particular bug being illustrated in that even Miss Cameron was laid low, a happening

'The Tempest' 1972.

hitherto thought to be impossible. One popular innovation at this time was the inauguration of conferences at which parents might meet the relevant staff to discuss their daughters' progress (or lack of it).

Nineteen seventy-four saw the retirement of two great contributors to the school. Joan Marchant had taught for many years and directed many noteworthy productions, adapting classics to the stage and giving the girls a wide range of drama. Doreen Campbell had been at the school for forty years. She had set and demanded from others the highest standards in everything that was done, in work, in discipline and in behaviour. Her magical conjuring of design and inspired use of colour and drapery had lifted many Moreton productions into the professional class, Never wishing to be in the limelight, she was always there working in the wings and backstage – a calm and comforting presence.

The school was sixty years old in 1973. Always over these years – and beyond – it retained the family atmosphere built up by the Lloyd-Williams clan; the ethos continued through all the changes and chances. There was a consciousness of the past, of the little traditions which were maintained through the generations. Carols in the Hall might no longer be in the Hall but there was a pleasing consciousness that this happy candle-lit Christmas ritual was part of the fabric of the school. All schools of course are different from each other but there was something special about the little kingdom of Moreton, lying in the Shropshire fields, a school which – at its best – encouraged the virtues of friendliness, courtesy, concern for others, liveliness of imagination and breadth of vision – and was not without a streak of eccentricity. Looking back, one Old Moretonian remembers a particular moment when – remarkably – she had risen at 5am to revise, sitting in the outdoor theatre. As the sun rose, she was suddenly struck by the beauty of her surroundings and the consciousness of the good fortune which had placed her as a member of this remarkable community with its endearing way of life nourished by its roots in the past. It was a quasi-spiritual experience. Another Old Moretonian, Head Prefect in her day, wrote in the School Diary: 'Sunday 5th July. My last day at Moreton! It's very sad that it is all over. We had the end of term service. It was terribly sad saying good-bye to everyone. I have enjoyed my seven years at Moreton and am very proud to be a Moretonian.'

VII A CORNER TURNED – JIM FIXES IT

I n the summer term of 1975, a sub-committee of Governors set about the task of selecting a new Principal. There was no preference as between a man or woman; only a desire to seek the best candidate. From more than a hundred enquirers, a short list was made, interviews conducted and the full body of Governors made their choice – E. J. Cussell, a graduate of Trinity College, Dublin and the holder of a Diploma of Education from Cambridge. His present post was that of Director of the Lycée des Nations International School, Geneva, having previously been Headmaster of a Preparatory School at Bishops Stortford. He was married to Georgina and they had three early teenage children, Sandra, Susan and Andrew.

So Moreton Hall acquired its first Headmaster – a considerable innovation for a school which had previously been directed by ladies for more than sixty years – at a time of impending crisis, the number of girls in the school having declined sharply to 219. It would take a considerable effort to get the institution back on course. It soon became obvious that the new Principal was an organisations man and an ambitious one at that. After some months he defined for his Governors his conclusions as to the strengths and weaknesses of the school – with considerable perception.

Jim Cussell.

The strengths he considered were the actual place itself with its beautiful setting in the countryside: the atmosphere in which staff and girls moved: the confidence and sense of responsibility which he found in the senior girls: the strengths of music and drama: the excellent standard of spoken English and the emphasis placed upon this subject: the strength of the school games and the outstanding record of the lacrosse teams: and the efficiency of the administrative back up.

On the other side of the coin was the idiosyncratic academic programme: the poor examination results in the GCE: considerable overstaffing: some weak teaching: lack of adequate teaching materials: an inadequate programme of recreation: weekends devoid of worthwhile activity: and a general lack of stimulation to encourage girls to higher levels in various fields and particularly the academic.

Obviously the first priority was to increase the number of pupils without whom the school would crumble away. The aim was to have 250 girls and a staff reduced to twenty-five, which would still leave a quite generous ratio of one to ten. The number of foreign girls should be reduced to ten per cent. Admirable as the efforts of Bronwen Lloyd-Williams had been to attract pupils from all over the world, the proportion had become too great at twenty-six per cent including fifty-five girls whose first language was not English. The attempt to attract day girls should be renewed. A major effort was to be made to improve public relations, urging parents and friends to help in this; a new prospectus was required: the press must be kept informed of Moreton activities: the educational agencies, like Gabbitas, must be alerted to the charms of the school. At the same time, when possible, a building programme must be undertaken to make up some of the deficiencies both in living space and teaching space.

It was with all these thoughts and plans in mind that Jim Cussell faced his first Parents' Weekend in the summer of 1976, the first appearance on the platform also of the new Chairman. The Principal's message was strong and confident. The weekend passed happily with the dancing of The Young Person's Guide to the Orchestra, choreographed by Janet Norton: a performance of Brecht's The Caucasian Chalk Circle and, for relaxation after such a stern test, the fun and frolic of The Boyfriend.

The absolutely essential reduction of numbers of teaching staff was a priority second only to the need to increase the numbers of pupils. But, as anyone who knows schools is well aware, it is practically impossible to sack a teacher. Jim Cussell actually did so on a couple of occasions – it had obviously not been a good idea for Latin to be taught by a Spaniard whose English was not perfect and whose temperament smacked of the Mediterranean. Both

Georgina and Jim Cussell (right).

cases went to an Industrial Tribunal. Winkling out unsatisfactory teachers was a slow process however successfully Jim Cussell conjured the appointments and retirements and in 1980 he was telling his Governors that he still had three less than satisfactory teachers. It was almost unbelievable that the school had a staff/pupil ratio of one to seven, a figure far in excess of the national average. Of course amongst much mediocrity there was some excellent teaching in certain subject areas; true to tradition, Moreton was strong in the arts – in English (though this was patchy), in history and in politics; but science was a disaster area. In 1976 three girls took science papers at 'A' level; there were three failures, three D grades and two E grades.

Part of the trouble was that the expectations were low. For many years the aim of the school was to provide a good liberal education with emphasis on literature, ballet, good deportment, music, correct speech – and skill at lacrosse – without pressure of examination results. Now the situation was changing, girls were looking forward to careers, the various womens' movements of the day were having their effect even on far away Moreton, and academic results were playing a greater part in an increasingly competitive world. It was not enough to say – as was frequently said or implied in Principals' reports – that results were much as expected – a peculiarly vacuous phrase. Although girls had obtained places at universities it was soon no longer to be the case that grades of one C and two Ds at 'A' level would get you a place for a non-academic degree course at, say, Reading University. Even

Jim Cussell was guilty of euphemism when he described the 1978 'A' level results as 'generally very good' when thirty-one girls could only produce seven A grades between them.

The combined results of three years – 1973, 1974, 1975 – for which the Governors called, were startling. At 'O' level there were 665 subjects passed and 714 failed: at 'A' level thirty-three per cent of subjects were failed, taking the grades A to C as constituting a pass, as generally recognised. To secure improvement was a long, hard road. Clearly too many subjects at 'O' level were being taken and effort was spread too widely. The curriculum was narrowed, with fewer options. More supervision of progress was instituted. Time had to be reallocated, with more periods for Maths and Science. Confidence in the Sixth Form had to be built up – early leavers left only nine girls in the Upper Sixth in 1976. And of course, the staff as well as the pupils had to be encouraged to aim higher and the dead wood eliminated.

The pressure exerted by Jim Cussell certainly brought results in the long run – but it was a very long run. He charted progress year by year and it was always upwards, but the starting base had been low. As late as 1982 only two girls obtained places at British universities; two at American universities. Four had to re-take their 'A' levels – this from a total of twenty girls. There were of course the occasional stars – a place at Cambridge in 1976 and another in 1980. It could be done.

In one vital sphere Jim Cussell was really successful – in building up the numbers and therefore in relaxing the financial pressure. In 1980, after his first five years, numbers had increased from 216 to 298, including six day girls. Confidence had really built, encouraged by the Principal's obvious energy and commitment. The parents were kept fully informed by frequent newsletters, the school magazine had a re-birth and appeared in attractive format, more lively in content and fully illustrated, and the Governors' files were filled not only with the minutes of numerous meetings but with papers on academic progress, backed up with graphs and occasional papers on philosophy of the school and plans for the immediate and the long term future. An Open Day was held. Much was owed in this flurry of activity to David Pilkington, Chairman of the Policy, Finance and General Purposes Committee, who steered with a firm but sensitive hand.

Despite the increase in income from extra numbers, the Governors had to pursue a tortuous financial path. In the late 1970s the overdraft could rise to £220,000 in August, the worst month in the year for all schools. This had to be serviced and the loan taken out to build the swimming pool – opened in 1978 – (the big splash) had to be repaid. However the school was beginning to make a healthy surplus on the annual revenue account. But further building, eagerly pressed by the Principal, would require further borrowing and careful diplomacy with the bank. In all this work the school was extremely fortunate to have the expertise and industry of John Knight; there were some tricky interviews with the bank manager in which the Chairman also took part. It became plain that if Moreton was to have the facilities it badly needed, it was necessary to carry a considerable load of debt. If on the other hand one waited cautiously until one had the money, the school might wither away.

Accordingly it was decided to build a new library (which should contain classrooms), a design centre and an enlargement to the dining hall. The architects were to be the Chris Cowen Partnership. The money was to be raised by a loan but another appeal was to be launched, this time of a different character as Jim Cussell took upon himself the role of Appeal Director, the Appeal mechanism to be wholly run in and by the school – another burden for the ever-willing Joan Pennington, who was the Appeal Secretary. A committee of parents was assembled in a advisory capacity. On account of much well planned activity and through the remarkable generosity of the majority of parents and friends a total of £130,000 was raised, much of it covenanted which, though very welcome, did bring cash flow problems.

Some excitement was generated by the offer of an African chief who had two girls in the school, to provide £80,000 which would pay for the Design Centre. Jim Cussell was the only person actually to meet the Chief but such was his enthusiasm and confidence that he persuaded the Governors, rather reluctantly, to invite him to join their body as representing the overseas parents. Members looked forward to meeting this somewhat mysterious figure but he never attended a meeting; even more eagerly Jim Cussell looked forward to the always promised and about to be delivered cheque – but, alas, it proved a chimera. The Chief's daughters left for Millfield and nothing more was heard.

VIII EXPANSION

The successful erection of the three new buildings was a great boost to confidence in the future of the school. It enabled a considerable redistribution of space, making for better conditions in teaching and accommodation and better amenities for staff. The loans which made all possible, it is true, hung heavily round the necks of the Governors but with careful management over several years, it was possible to see the way ahead. In 1977 Miss Sylvia Lloyd-Williams died, to be followed shortly afterwards by Miss Betty (Mrs Brett). They had always maintained their connection to the school and were the last of 'Aunt Lil's' nine daughters to die. Each left legacies to the school and about the same time Bronwen's estate was at last cleared up and £8000 came to Moreton from that source. By good fortune the owner of the land adjoining the school, which was between the back of the school and the railway line, wanted to sell and after negotiations conducted by Toby Salway, this area was bought, thus pushing out the school boundary to what, in a sense, was its natural limit. Another loan was taken out to pay for this.

One area of concern to Jim Cussell – which was not new – was the whole matter of pastoral care, increasingly so as the number of girls mounted. The four Houses (or Setts) into which the girls were divided were artificial in that they had no physical base and operated purely for competitive purposes. There were House Tutors in various areas adjacent to the dormitories but their duties were custodial rather than pastoral and could not be equated with Housemistresses in other schools. Occasionally there were House Tutors who were effective in their role but it was not easy to find single women who found this responsibility attractive, especially as the living quarters were generally minimalist. In fact, one or two curious characters are remembered, one who, after the girls were asleep, used to serenade them through the dormitories with the violin; one night she even had them out on the games fields in their night attire for no particular reason, to be irritably sent back by the awoken Principal in dressing gown attire and dressing down mode. This lady did not long continue. It became the aim to provide decent living quarters for those with this important responsibility and to turn them into Housemistresses as generally understood. For a time Housemothers were sought who had no teaching responsibility but this experiment was short lived.

Jim Cussell invented a School Council as a consultative body in order to try and bring together various elements in the school for discussion of the general machinery by which the institution was run; this in addition to Prefects' Meetings. Jim chaired the Council: the Vice-Principal belonged as did representatives from both the teaching staff and the administrative staff, kitchen and matrons. Girls were represented by members of each form from Sixth to Transitional. Jim tried hard to make it a positive and constructive body – though emphasising that it had no executive power – but, as is the way of such bodies in schools, it tended to be a focus of complaints. Once more the eternal subject of how to get the school into and out of the dining hall and what happened when they were in there, featured largely. Increasingly there were complaints about insufficient food, especially in the evening. The younger age group clamoured for more outings and for more walks (on which they had to be conducted). More shopping leaves were requested; the timing and extent of exeats was discussed: and, as ever, questions as to what dress could be worn when and where.

In fact the matter of food became so important that Moreton's one and only strike took place. In the dining hall, the whole school refused to eat; after an interval every girl walked out. Jim Cussell was not pleased and summoned the Prefects to his House where they turned up en bloc without a single blackleg. It was an unexpected and rather distasteful event but showed the strength of feeling on this subject. Some changes followed.

The subject of weekend activities was another area concerning which there was frequent complaint. Jim was only too aware of the problem, which is common to boarding schools everywhere. But at Moreton the ghosts of 'Aunt Lil' and Miss Mary were still present, giving Sunday a puritan touch: church in the morning – generally at Gobowen – two hours on the bed rest in the afternoon, evening service in the school at 6pm which meant that those on exeat had to return by that time. Saturday too was a blank day for many. Those in school teams were busy but there was not much for the others although the Prefects organised informal dancing in the gym to the gramophone and there was an occasional lecture. With most of the staff being non-resident, it was not easy to organise activities though attempts were made. One contribution was the building of a small golf course – Jim's brother was a golf professional. The number of walks was increased, Weston

Rhyn being a favourite destination because of the telephone kiosk there.

In 1979 two incidents served as reminders that Moreton was not entirely isolated from the developing world. One night a girl was the victim of a sexual assault in her bedsit by an intruder who was later caught and sentenced; and a girl brought cannabis into the school with intent to use it. Fortunately this was almost immediately brought to notice and the offender summarily dealt with, parents being fully informed in each case.

By 1980 Jim Cussell's attempts to reduce the numbers on the staff were proving successful and a new salary structure had been agreed. Whereas in 1975 salaries had formed sixty-four per cent of the gross fee income, this figure was reduced to fifty-five per cent by 1980. In that year Geoffrey Smales was appointed as Director of Studies; his rigorous and industrious approach did much to re-shape the curriculum and to deploy his colleagues most advantageously. The 1980s saw the retirement of several figures familiar to Moretonians over the years. Merriel Halsall-Williams had already moved on though this was not to be the end of her connection with Moreton. She had done much, particularly for drama and in the sphere of spoken English. Year after year girls showed exceptional results in the Oxford Certificate of Oral English and in the examinations of the English Speaking Board. A Moreton Public Speaking Team had been runners-up in a competition involving schools from all over the country. Ursula Green had for no less than thirty-five years taught the piano and made a big contribution to the music department. Another of those who seemed perpetually present and who retired at this time was Ursula Roberts, for many years Librarian, and, in her quiet way, a tower of strength, whose talents were spread over a wide field of school life and one whose links went back to Bronwen's early days. Her industry had done much for the Old Moretonians' Association.

Tony Pahlen (the Baron) had taught for twenty years and Bob Coutts for fifteen. The latter had taught most subjects from Economics to Greek and both had contributed greatly to Common Room life. It was a surprise, though it should not really have been unexpected, when Janet Norton announced her wish to give up the direction and teaching of gym, dance and games. Thirty years was a long time to hold this onerous position, so important to the Moreton ethos. She continued her work as Vice-Principal, teaching biology and divinity and would devote time to liaison with Old Moretonians.

New appointments which were to have a considerable effect were of David Lloyd to teach geography and Michael Hartley, chemistry; two others who were to give much to Moreton were Trish Fenwick and Sally Tester, while the coming of Evelyn Davies led to much needed development in the area of pastoral care. Evelyn Davies was a trained counsellor and a remedial teacher.

With help from others a life skills course was set up and General Studies reorganised. Evelyn taught divinity; she was later ordained in the Church of England. A wave of matrimony swept the staff at this time. Two members became Mr and Mrs Cadwallader and Margery Gilder, Kay Jackson and Sue Lea all aroused a buzz of chatter amongst their pupils as they made their respective ways to the altar.

Bob Knill, Peter Heywood, Geoff Smales, Keith Hunter.

In 1980 the Governors decided to do what they had long wished – to build a house for the Principal. The flat in which the family lived was very inadequate for a family of three growing children. They had not at first found it easy to settle. Weston Rhyn was not Geneva. But by now Moreton had become home and it was only right that adequate living accommodation should be provided. Although full of good intent, the Governors were tied down by their financial position, in that the overdraft and loan interest had to be paid – a large annual sum, the interest rate being seventeen per cent, despite the much improved school income. Nonetheless the decision was taken and it was hoped that at least part of the cost would be paid by interest free loans from parents and this indeed did provide a much improved cash flow. But then there intervened a Dutch parent, Mr Vlissingen with an offer of an unusual kind. If the school rented the site of the new house to him, he would pay for the building (paying a small ground rent) and the school would buy the house back from him over a period of five years, paying as interest annually eight per cent of the house cost. Thus Capital Gains Tax was avoided and the school given a vital breathing space in which to accumulate the necessary sum. This ingenious scheme was negotiated with Mr Vlissingen by John Knight who twice travelled to Holland to negotiate it. ('The Treaty of Utrecht.') It was a good bargain for all concerned and the cost of the house

£96,000, was punctually paid off by 1986. The vacant Principal's flat was occupied by Mr and Mrs Norman and she became a Housemistress, living centrally in the school.

The new 'Toblerone' Boarding House.

IX LIFE IN THE '80s

n 1982, the Governors – urged strongly by the Principal – made the decision to build a new boarding house. The need was obvious; with increased numbers in the school there was pressure from all directions, but particularly on boarding space, the numbers having risen by nearly a hundred since Jim Cussell took over. How could this large expenditure be undertaken, the school overdraft still being substantial? It was decided once more that there should be an Appeal, as before run in-house, with the Principal as Director; and the bank agreed to a loan of £700,000 to be repaid over ten years. Once more much was owed to John Knight's negotiating powers and to the general strength of the revenue account. It was also decided that when the new house was built, it would be feasible to plan for a total of 320/325 girls – without increasing the staff. There was without doubt greater confidence in the school, which ten years previously had seemed in danger of collapse. The threat of political interference from the Labour Government had waned.

So the Chris Cowen Partnership went to work and produced a very original plan which turned itself into what was to be universally called the 'Toblerone', with an A frame of timber imported from Scandinavia. Through hard work, the Appeal went well and the building was ready for use in 1985. So it was possible to implement a logical internal organisation with six Houses each with Housemistress and Matron. It was intended that this should also mean a vertical structure of different year groups in each House instead of the then horizontal arrangement whereby each House contained girls of the same age. However this change was never implemented. The junior age groups went into the new building, at first called North and South Houses, later Norton and Roberts and then Norton-Roberts. But there were to be Sixth Form girls in each House, each spending two out of the six Sixth Form terms there, to act in a general supervisory capacity and to see that the Sixth Form did not get isolated from the rest of the school. The increase in numbers was not slow; 308 in 1982 (including thirty-four day girls) became 334 in 1987 (including twenty day girls). The only disappointing feature was that only six per cent of these girls were of foreign origin. Once it was felt the proportion was too large; now it was too small, although there were more than fifty daughters of expatriates. Possibly the decrease in foreign girls had something to do with the Thatcher policy of making them pay full university fees. Meanwhile the academic results improved year by year and were now perfectly respectable though still it could be said that expectations were not high enough and few made any impression on Oxford and Cambridge, despite an Exhibition to St Hilda's, Oxford in 1982.

Ambitious as ever, Jim Cussell next turned his attention and that of the Governors to the need for a sports hall, with ancillary tennis courts. Preliminary discussion suggested that one million pounds would be needed and the Governors hastily adjourned for lunch. The school was, as usual, fully stretched financially and there was much refurbishing to be done in living accommodation to bring the rest of the school up to the Toblerone standard. It was decided at this time that the Transitional form (those under eleven) should be abolished as being a rather awkward appendage to a school of 330 with a Sixth Form of nearly one hundred. Interestingly the Transitional came back as Moreton First a dozen years later.

Ursula Green, Richard Stephens, Rosemary Brown, Kenneth Brown.

In 1986 Malcolm Mitchell, a solicitor in Shrewsbury, began his stint as Chairman of the Council, which has continued ever since. After a major contribution over the years, David Pilkington retired and John Matthews, a parent of three Moreton daughters, took on the Chairmanship of the Policy, Finance and General Purposes Committee. Toby Salway retired. He had borne the heat and burden under three Principals who had turned to him on all matters to do with buildings, maintenance and property. Few have served the school with greater devotion and the same was true of Dr Pat Salt who retired from his position as school doctor. A spasm of anxiety went through the school when Jim Cussell became ill with an, at first, undiagnosed condition which was found to stem from a pineal gland. He was absent for some months but returned wholly fit. However Janet Norton's health was deteriorating, leading to her resignation, at the age of fifty-five, in 1985. She had been at the very heart of Moreton for thirty-three years and given a wonderful example of energy and commitment, not only in exercising her own particular talents on the games field and in dance and ballet, but in her general overseeing of the school from her position as Vice-Principal. Sadly she had only a few months to enjoy retired life in her lovely cottage. Chirk Church was entirely filled by her many friends at her Memorial Service.

There was always a fear that a school which had grown so rapidly might lose that particular family atmosphere which was Moreton's outstanding characteristic. The Principal was very much alive to this danger and did all he could to maintain and improve pastoral care. The new house system considerably helped; Tutor Groups were established and non-resident staff were encouraged to participate in extra-curricular activity. Whereas lacrosse remained central in games organisation, there was more emphasis on other sports – hockey was introduced, there was more opportunity for tennis particularly after Steve Welti came as coach and for the first time, athletics. Bronwen had always opposed this activity for undisclosed reasons to do with the development of girls' bodies (though she encouraged them to twist themselves into unlikely shapes in Greek dancing). Entries were also made for the Duke of Edinburgh awards. In 1981 computers were introduced: and with the arrival of Mark Wright on the staff a whole new area was opened up with the establishment of Moreton Enterprises – a properly constituted company with officers and shareholders which first transformed the Tuck Shop, opened up a sub-branch of the Midland Bank and spread to Moreton Travel (a minibus was bought) and

Janet Norton

then a seventeen acre farm, followed by the taking of local opinions as regards reopening local railway stations. This caused a little flutter of publicity. Mark Wright was also one of a team working under Evelyn Davies which set up a thorough going career advisory body.

The Principal caused a major sensation when at a staff meeting in 1983 he made a long pre-meditated announcement – that he proposed to introduce Saturday morning school; a stunned silence followed. Jim had been urged by his Chairman for some time to take this step. No boarding school has a complete holiday on Saturday and on Sunday and valuable teaching time was unfilled. In fact this change was not implemented for two years to enable staff to get used to the idea, to plan how to use the time and to allow the objectors to resign. Non-academic subjects were to be taught on Saturday from 9am to 11am and there was to be time for music, art and other occupations. Only two staff members objected at the very end. At the same time Wednesday afternoons were to be devoted to cultural activities, making a good break from academic work.

The appointment of a Vice-Principal in Janet's stead was unfortunately not successful. For a time there was no Vice-Principal and Judy Roe, head of social studies, who had a long and remarkable record of successful teaching, and Dr Mike Ingle, a scientist, successfully held the fort before the appointment of Mrs Patricia Gregson in 1987. Two newcomers just before this time were Hilary Prescott,

Margery Gilder, Trish Fenwick.

starting a long record of service, and Michael Manby, the recently retired Headmaster of Prestfelde Prep School, who came to help out temporarily in the English department and stayed and stayed. Another appointment of 1987 was that of Mrs Radford to take charge of the catering department; her predecessor Ann Beere, had made a remarkable transformation in this vital area, including lunch on a 'flexi system' which really meant a cafeteria meal. One disadvantage was that a girl could miss a meal without being noticed. The punishment was dire: to sit at a separate table for the whole of the meal (forty minutes) for a month.

During these years of the 1980s the old high standards were not achieved in drama owing to staff changes, though Richard Stephens gave a lead in music. Other activities flourished: there was a most successful lacrosse tour to the USA – only one match lost: there were expeditions to the continent with serious intent of learning languages: the standard of Spoken English was as high as ever (five open awards at one of the Crewe Festivals).

Minutes of prefects' meetings record the usual discussions; the dining hall does not feature so frequently, though the Principal is recorded as being 'appalled' when he heard that senior girls were tripping up junior girls on the way out. There were complaints about deportment, still an important feature while Janet Norton was around. ('The school needs to sit up'.) As was usual with prefects the Lower Sixth were criticised for their unhelpful attitude. One thing the prefects did enjoy were their weekly tea parties to which a couple of members of the staff were invited; and immense energy was put into writing and performing the annual end of term Prefects' Song.

Jim Cussell's relations with his Upper Sixth were not always happy and he confessed as much in his Parents' Day speech of 1984. He fully understood the importance of the pastoral side of the school and frequently wrote about it; but his own strengths did not lie in this area. He relaxed some of the restrictions, particularly in clothing, and gave increased privileges to the Upper Fifth, rightly realising that girls (and boys) were growing up physically much faster than their predecessors. His liberalism even stretched to allowing, for a time, a smoking room for Upper Sixth girls who had their parents' consent. But often he was giving talks to the senior girls about their general behaviour and attitudes, particularly before dances when boys came from Shrewsbury, Ellesmere and Concord College and the twin threats of smoking and drinking had to be countered, not always with success.

Upstairs, Governors may govern and staff may teach but what of the world viewed from downstairs? Every head prefect was enjoined to keep a school diary. This document was generally no more than a list of events, day by day. But occasionally a head prefect would add her own frank comments so that we get a warts-and-all view. Here are some extracts, splendidly incongruous, with national events mixed with local scandals:

> 'Mrs Cadwallader fell in the pool while teaching canoeing!'
> 'President Sadat was mortally wounded.'
> 'My brother came to visit with a friend of his (what excitement!).'
> 'S– B– ate ten Weetabix.'
> 'Cussell had a real go at the Sixth Form: he was angry because L– had been doing very naughty things with her boyfriend on the golf course.'

'Mrs D– got her blouse caught in Miss Pennington's paper shredder! She had to be cut free.'

'England have attacked Argentina in the Falklands.'

'K– B– ate 14 pieces of toast, having previously complained to the caterer that they were not done properly.'

'(At a dance) a few boys seemed to have lost their trousers and were dancing in the extension in their boxers. Some of the boring Lower Sixth were surprisingly rampant.'

'Laker Airlines went bust.'

'Early church was taken by that boring old Vicar.'

'T– broke J– s thumb as she was trying her out on self defence.'

'Cussell threatened (three girls) with suspension for "smooching" at the   dance unless evidence could be produced to the contrary so panic set in and twenty other girls all owned up to smooching, so Cussell didn't know what to do.'

Despite all these excitements however, the terms passed not unhappily, the prefects doing their various tasks as of yore, electing committees, teaching the new girls the school anthem, Gaude Plebs, and explaining the myriad bounds rules. The Advent wreath was made: Cocked Hat Sunday was celebrated: the Nativity Play took place before Christmas, there were Carols in the Hall, according to tradition. The school year came to an end. 'Packing mainly in the morning. After lunch final prayers and distribution of certificates: I burst into tears – what a scene. Thank you Moreton for the past four years, I'll be back to see you all.'

X CRISIS SURMOUNTED

Numbers in the school reached 348 (including twenty-four day girls) in 1988 which proved to be a high water mark. There were eighty taking the entrance examination. Encouraged by this the Governors felt it was possible to embark on building the sports hall. With only one loan – that for the 'Toblerone' – outstanding, a new loan was taken out, the bank now having confidence in the future of the school. At the same time another Appeal was to be launched, the third, the others having been in 1978 and 1984. This was to be run from the school, the Principal again taking on the role of Director. His energy and initiative, supported by a group of parents, led to a successful outcome, £225,000 being raised. It was noticeable that, as previously, parents were the main contributors, support from Old Moretonians being disappointing. Why do Old Boys support their schools with much greater enthusiasm than Old Girls?

The sports hall construction went smoothly and within budget; the contractors were Pochin Ltd. The school were greatly helped by one Governor, Peter Drew, (as with the new boarding house), he having experience and expertise as the Chairman of a development and building company in London. The sports hall was indeed a major project which included the construction of three tennis courts and provided facilities for badminton, basketball, netball and volleyball; it could be turned into an assembly hall to seat a thousand. Very important too was the provision of changing accommodation – every girl had a locker – so that the unsatisfactory system of changing in houses came to an end. In January 1990 the hall was ready for use; the Sports Minister was engaged to open it but sadly the extreme weather and its effect on rail travel made it impossible for him to leave London. As soon as the hall was open, attention was turned on the gym to refurbish and re-equip it as a a centre for music, drama and art. To celebrate its new life it was called the Musgrave Centre.

Mike Ingle, the new Director of Studies, wasted no time in getting down to a detailed examination of the curriculum and timetable. In 1988 the results of the GCSE (recently introduced) at 'O' level were quite good. At 'A' level, though the best results for a decade, the standard of performance overall was not high, fifty-three per cent passing in the A to C grades, generally recognised as a pass. There were only six A grades from forty-four girls, though thirteen entered universities that year. The bright girls were certainly doing better and a couple of years later five candidates obtained places at Cambridge. The Ingle review led to a new structure of the school day which now ended – so far as academic teaching was concerned – at 4pm. There were still nine periods in the day; was the timetable too full? was there over-teaching, which visiting inspectors had suggested? At any rate there was now a much more logical structure to the week.

In 1988 the school marked its seventy-fifth birthday. In October a general celebration took place and a service was held at which Canon Peter Delaney, a Governor, gave a moving address. The manifold activities of the school were to be seen and recorded in a magazine of record proportions. Particularly striking to many were the various activities of Moreton Enterprises, a limited company which had a £20,000 turnover and ran a recognised sub-branch of the Midland Bank. Apart from the shop, Enterprises ran the payphones and later the fax machines in the school. Another activity was the farm where seventeen acres were looked after and where there were sheep, pigs and goats. Moreton Transport too, had really taken off – the only British Rail ticket agency located in a school The annual special train, entirely organised by the girls, carried seven hundred passengers to a chosen attractive town – Bath or York – and every ticket was sold.

Training for business.

Out of a geography project run by David Lloyd had grown the Village Stations Project in which the girls set out to find if there was a local demand for the re-opening or construction of village stations in the area. Whittington was a place where it seemed there was a demand and Moreton Transport was soon embroiled with both British Rail and the local planning authority.

Another activity which had expanded considerably under the direction of Hilary Prescott was community service. ('Granny bashing' as it was known at a nearby boys' school.) Much was done with and for the adjacent Derwen Centre for the disabled.

At the seventy-fifth celebration the art exhibition included a mother-and-daughter display by Denise Rylands and her daughter Alison. Drama was now in the hands of Karin Wegener. The Fauré Requiem was sung this year but, although there were 158 music lessons every week (half of them piano) and girls duly passed their Associated Board examinations, it was impossible to have a full school orchestra owing to the shortage of string players. The shortage was exacerbated by the violin teacher being wedded to the Suzuki method, then so popular, which was fine for starting very young players but was not very successful for later development.

The arrival of Mrs Patricia Gregson as Vice-Principal greatly added to the central direction and control of the school. With much experience behind her, she radiated a very steadying influence and made it clear that she was approachable by all. Once when taking a staff meeting her conduct of the discussion was so brisk and brief that some of her colleague, used to the Cussell verbiage, gave her a round of applause.

There were two resignations at this time, both of them much regretted. Brother Ronald an Anglican Franciscan monk, had somehow become part of the community in an undefined role. He was called the Religious-in-Residence and radiated a remarkable idiosyncratic influence over the school society; ill health had led to his withdrawal to his monastery. For the same cause, Evelyn Davies felt compelled to retire at this time. Her work had been wide ranging including remedial work, counselling, careers advice and the teaching of religious studies. She was later ordained and devoted much of her life to helping cancer sufferers.

From what seemed a clear blue sky, the Autumn term of 1990 brought with it tragedy and crisis. The Chairman of the Governors, Malcolm Mitchell, who acted with astonishing speed and wisdom, describes the incidents of an October weekend:

> Early in 1990 the Governors felt that Jim Cussell and Georgina were both showing signs of stress and looked as if they needed a

rest. We suggested that they should go away for the Autumn Term for a sabbatical. They gratefully agreed, and at the end of term off they went with farewells and best wishes and 'see you in January'. Jim said that they did not have any particular plans but would start off living in their flat in London.

The idea was that in Jim's absence Mrs Pat Gregson would be Acting Principal. She had shown herself to be a highly efficient Deputy and none of us had any doubts that she would be well able to see the school through until January.

Some time during the summer holidays, probably early August, Jim telephoned me at my office and asked if he could come to see me. He said that he would rather not say why until he arrived. We arranged to meet, and he came down from London to Shrewsbury for the purpose.

When he arrived he sat down and said straight out 'Malcolm, my resignation is on the table. I have been having an affair with Pat. Pat knows that I am coming to see you about it.'

My response was to say 'Hold it, hold it, we must talk this though. First, who knows about it?' 'Only Joan', Joan being Joan Franklin.

'Where do you think the affair is heading?' I asked.

'I don't know, I'm deeply confused, I'm having counselling.'

After talking things over with him I took the view that it was too soon to make any decisions. So much might change in a couple of months. If the affair were to fizzle out then it might be possible for the Cussells to return in January, which might or might not require Pat Gregson to leave. If the affair were to continue . . . but best for the moment to wait and see.

I decided that I needed to know whether it was true that only Joan knew. Joan thought that no-one else did know: it seemed to be a well-kept secret so far. The first step was to find out whether one or two other key people knew. The obvious first person to see was a senior member of the staff. I invited myself out to see her. After making polite conversation over a cup of tea I threw out a few bits of bait to see if she would rise to them, but the reaction was clear – she did not make any connections with anything which she knew. A couple of telephone calls to other people similarly produced no reactions. No-one else did know. So it was a matter of wait and see.

When term started I went out a couple of times to see Pat.

Much was reassuring. She was being a thoroughly competent stand-in and it was gratifying to see signs that staff and girls alike were regarding her with affectionate respect. As for the affair, Pat said that she did not know where it was all heading – she was conscious that Jim was in a state of totally confused uncertainty and she confirmed that he was undergoing counselling. She herself had hopes that she and Jim had a future together but Jim was in no fit condition to consider that future rationally – let alone to make any decisions. At the end of September she told me that she was going down to London that weekend to see Jim and would tell me about it the following week.

That Saturday was the annual Old Salopian gathering in Shrewsbury. My wife, Judy, and I had signed on for the dinner, to be preceded by drinks in our old Houses.

I was just getting out of the bath to dress and go to Ridgemount when the telephone rang. Judy answered and called me to the phone. In fact there were two calls in quick succession and I cannot clearly recall which came first – Jim or Joan Franklin. Judy says that it was Jim. Anyway, the messages were that Pat was dead, Jim was in a state of tearful collapse and now he was unequivocally resigning. What had happened was not made clear to me but in outline there had been some scene between them after which Pat had taken some pills and drunk a large amount of alcohol. She had been taken to hospital and there she had died.

I set about telephoning other Governors to tell them what had happened and said that I would let them know as soon as I had heard more. The question in the short term was who was to act as Principal, since it would be unwise and unfair to ask Mike Ingle (Director of Studies) or Judy Roe (elder stateswoman) to take charge. By the time I had rung as many of the Governors as were home there seemed little more that I could do for the moment. I had missed drinks in Ridgemount but there was still time to go to the dinner and no reason why not to. And I wanted to consult the Shrewsbury Headmaster, Ted Maidment – not a Governor at Moreton, but someone to consult anyway. Similarly my neighbour Richard Raven, the Second Master, would have some useful thoughts.

By the end of the evening I had a list of no fewer than four recently-retired Heads in the area who might be asked to stand in. The front-runner was Michael Maloney, who had actually been at the dinner as a former member of staff at Shrewsbury and was an experienced Headmaster.

On the Sunday morning I rang around the Governors again, I mentioned the list of potential Heads and asked for authority to proceed as I thought best starting with Michael Maloney They all agreed. I rang him next and asked if I could come out and have a chat with him at home in Chirbury on an educational subject. He asked when, and I said 'How about now? Shall I come out right now?' He said that would be fine, and out I went.

When we had got over the re-introductions and had settled down I asked him if he fancied the idea of filling in as Principal at Moreton for an interregnum. 'When are we talking about?' 'How about starting tomorrow morning?' I explained the reasons. In a few minutes we had agreed, although inevitably there would be practicalities to be discussed in the days ahead.

I rang Joan at Moreton and reported on progress. I said that Michael Maloney and I would wish to see all staff in the staff room first thing on Monday morning and that he and I would then address the whole school at morning assembly. She and I agreed that we needed to get a letter out to parents that day if possible. Judy and I drove to Moreton and the three of us prepared the letter and duplicated it and got it into envelopes for posting. The gist of the letter was that Pat had tragically died in circumstances that were not clear but would give rise to an inquest, that Jim was not in a fit condition to return and that we had arranged for the reins to be taken temporarily by a certain Mr Michael Maloney who was ideally qualified for the task in that he had been and done this that and the other. Judy and I delivered the bag of letters to the back door of the post office headquarters in Shrewsbury and off they went, to be on the breakfast tables of parents on Monday morning. Copies also went to Governors with an extra note from me.

On Monday morning I spoke to the staff as arranged. For almost everyone there had been no warning of what had happened and the news came as a devastating shock. They had indeed been unaware of anything untoward happening between Jim and Pat and she had been very popular with them. There was no time for much more than a brief introduction of Michael with a promise of another visit within a day or two to talk things over further. For the moment they should please show their well-known loyalty and professionalism. On to the assembly.

A few of the day-children had been told of the letter by their parents, but the word had not generally got around far and the great majority were as unaware as the staff had been. I said briefly that I had terrible news for them: Mrs Gregson had died suddenly on the previous Saturday. She would be sadly missed by us all. Mr Cussell would not be able to return and here was their new Principal, Mr Maloney. He said a few words. I then left.

I drove back to my office, but by then my adrenalin had run out. I was in no condition to do anything but to go home and collapse.

A day or two later I did return for another meeting with staff. They were grateful for having been told as much as we knew at that stage. For those with long memories this was better than being given the more guarded information handed out on the death of Bron Lloyd-Williams. Parents apparently had approved of our actions and letter, but they had misunderstood my reference to Jim not being in a fit condition to return: perhaps quite naturally they had taken this as a reference to his physical health, suspecting that there had been a recurrence of the health problem which he had had a couple of years before. Staff suggested that another letter to parents could correct this suspicion and perhaps say a bit more. A second letter went out saying that until the inquest I would have to be guarded in what I said but that I could tell them that there was no problem over Jim's physical health: it was his mental state and his relationship with Pat which had led him to resign and so prevented his return. I said that we were all confident that the school community was so strong that it would ride the storm without difficulty.

The response from the entire Moreton family was superb – parents, staff and girls. The school seemed to sail on as if nothing had happened. Not a single girl either at the school or entered for the school was withdrawn. Parents appreciated having been kept informed and they made sure that nothing was said or done to harm the school's standing. The only mildly dissenting voices were from a few parents who thought that Governors should have encouraged Jim to return – but that truly had not been an option.

The remaining fear was about what might emerge at the inquest and what publicity might follow. In fact the inquest revealed very little other than the cause of death. The Coroner said that there was no evidence to suggest that Pat had intended to take her own life and that her death was accidental. As for the publicity, the inquest had been immediately preceded by an inquest on the death of a well-known singer from a slightly earlier age. A swarm of reporters were there for that reason but they all left the courtroom as soon as that inquest came to an end. A small and uninformative paragraph appeared some weeks later on an inner page of a local newspaper and that was that.

XI THE GREAT LEAP FORWARD

All were saddened that the contribution of Jim and Georgina Cussell should have this conclusion. When they arrived in 1976, Moreton was at a crossroads. If the numbers declined further it would hardly be possible to carry on the school; everything depended on the fee income – there was no other. The almost immediate build up of numbers owed everything to Jim's energy, his eloquence, his persuasive powers, his understanding of public relations and his general power of leadership. It very soon became obvious

Moreton First afloat.

that this was a school which was not standing still or living on its past reputation though he was very careful to nurture Moreton's particular virtues and the family atmosphere created over the years by the Lloyd-Williams family. He was a great forward planner and was constantly reviewing the position of the school and looking for the way ahead. In no sphere was this more obvious than in the remarkable building programme which took place over the fifteen years, propelling his Governors to take risks in the sure confidence that they would enable the school to grow and flourish. Grow it did. From 217 girls in 1975, the roll reached 348 in his last year. Gradually the academic standard rose, though he was disappointed it did not rise more quickly. Games continued to flourish and the lacrosse record was continued. Music and drama were encouraged and other activities introduced. Not all his staff appointments were a success but he brought many to Moreton who were to become pillars of the community. He was always conscious of keeping everyone in the picture – staff and parents; with the latter his relations were always good and he laboured with great commitment to make the three Appeals of his time successful and well over half a million pounds were raised in this way. It was very sad that it all had to end in tears. But he and Georgina had the satisfaction of knowing that they left a solidly founded community which could face the next years – when difficulties did arise – with confidence.

Michael Maloney's experience was wide. After teaching at Shrewsbury School he went to Eastbourne College, where he became Deputy Headmaster, going on from there to be Headmaster of Welbeck College, run by the army. There followed three years as Head of Kamuzu School, Malawi, one of Dr Banda's favourite projects. Before coming to Moreton he was doing consultancy work from his home in Powys. He was a scientist and a Scholar of Trinity College, Oxford. He was married to Jancis.

To take over a school without any notice whatever was a tall order. Obviously the priority was to establish confidence and he was much impressed by the reaction of staff and pupils to the tragedy. The Head Prefect wrote in her diary, 'Everyone is naturally totally distrait, however there is just nothing we can do except stick together and show our strength. Mr Maloney is going to be difficult to adjust to; ah, well, we'll just have to pull our weight.' It was a very proper and typical response.

The new Principal – and he was that – not Acting Principal, was fortunate to have at his side Joan Franklin with her great competence and wide experience; and John Knight could be relied on to steer the ship so far as the finances went. Dr Ingle and Judy Roe were not unused to responsibility. It was hoped that the new Bursar, already appointed, would give much needed help

The high life.

but unfortunately this appointment was not successful. Parents made clear their support and the new Principal had no worries on this score; he was amused to find that a number of fathers had been his pupils at Shrewsbury.

So the second half of the Michaelmas term was safely navigated. Mike Maloney warmed to the atmosphere of Moreton which he found friendly and welcoming. The Head Prefect again, 'Mr Maloney is a genuine sort of bloke who seems to have settled particularly well though his very direct manner initially quite shocked us! The thing I really like about him is that he doesn't stand for any nonsense. If he thinks someone should be expelled or punished, he will make damn sure that they get what they deserve without any faffing around.'

Another factor which made these times difficult and which the school had to face was an economic recession which was to have its effect on numbers, as did the now very common policy of most of the major boys' schools in opening their doors to girls – and not just in the Sixth Form. The decade of 1990s was to see a considerable decline in boarding numbers throughout the country.

Meanwhile the Governors set about finding a new Principal in the usual way – advertisements, checking on candidates and compiling a short list. The result was wholly disappointing. After interviewing those on the short list, the selection committee was unanimous in rejecting all applicants. They would have to try again; but obviously some time must elapse before a second effort, It was decided that Mike Maloney should be asked to stay on until the end of the summer term 1992, when he would have completed nearly two years and reached his own retiring age when he would be eligible for a pension.

Mike Maloney had the strong support of the Vice-Principal, Alison Scott, who had been a housemistress at Roedean. She only stayed for two years but was a source of strength at a difficult time – and difficult it certainly was. In September 1991 numbers had gone down to 305, a decrease of thirteen per cent from the preceding term. Mike Maloney was quick to see that the school was seriously over-staffed but quick action to remedy this was difficult, though he set about making such economies as were possible. That year the Governors were landed with an unwanted bill to renew the sewage system, not a matter that could wait.

In October 1991 the Governors' search for a new Principal came to an end and they were able to announce the coming, in September 1992, of Jonathan Forster. Educated at Shrewsbury School, he had taken his degree at Leeds University in English and taught at Hymers College, Hull, before in 1983 moving to Strathallan School as Head of English, where he had become the housemaster of a girls' house which had quickly expanded in size. Married to Paula, an English graduate, they had two daughters of nine and seven.

The prospect was in many ways daunting. In the new Principal's first term the numbers were down to 274 and were to drop further to a low of 267 – ninety girls fewer than in Jim Cussell's last year. In consequence the school's overdraft passed the agreed level by a substantial amount: the bank took alarm and called in Price Waterhouse, the accountants, to make a report – for which the school had to pay. Their representatives were disguised as 'educational consultants' so that there should not be too much alarm and they made a very thorough examination both of the accounts and of the school itself. Their report was not pessimistic in that they found the school to be flourishing and in good order but – as was obvious – there had to be a considerable scaling down to make a smaller school viable. There was also some rescheduling of loans and various recommendations for tighter financial control. But the plain fact which underlay the verbiage of the report was a very obvious one which did not need an accountant to point out – if numbers could be increased the school would flourish and if they declined much further there was unlikely to be a future.

Jonathan Forster set about his task with enormous enthusiasm and was soon well on the way to reviving confidence. His influence was felt throughout the school and beyond; parental interest revived and, although total numbers were low, at the end of his first year there were sixty new entrants – the most for several years. In his turn he and Paula were struck, as others had so often been, by the spirit of the place and the enthusiasm and high morale of the girls.

There were some hard decisions to be made as regards the staff; several became part-time and the deployment of teachers was studied so that the curriculum had a leaner look, while continuing to cover the essential subjects. Dr Ingle having retired, Mike Hartley, both a scholar and administrator with flair, became Head of Sixth Form studies, spearheading the thorough assessment of the academic programme. Jim Cussell had always praised his staff for their professionalism and hard work but whereas these words would apply to most, they did not apply to all and there were teaching weaknesses which had to be remedied. (Jim was given to falling into over-statement as when he told his Governors that Moreton was at the top of the First Division of Girls' Schools.) What was cheering in the new regime was that academic results improved considerably. In 1995 half the candidates achieved A or B grades at 'A' level – the best ever at Moreton – and there were ninety-seven per cent A to C passes at GCSE. There were four Oxbridge places in 1994.

The new Principal's obvious energy and commitment restored confidence in the school very quickly. The numbers were in the 260s for most years after 1994 which relieved financial worries, though the school was carrying a heavy burden of interest on the various loans from the past. Looking ahead there would have to be expenditure on Information Technology, the increasingly popular subject of Business Studies and – as often in the past – there was the hope that staff housing might make it possible to have more resident staff on the spot.

One area which needed attention was that of Moreton Enterprises which had grown enormously, fostered by Mark Wright. Girls had a real chance of being involved in serious business. The shop was the main centre of activity and income; the branch of the Midland Bank was operating an increasing number of accounts: the payphones (soon to be operated by cards) and the fax machines, when they were available, were organised: the minibus and its activities was owned by Enterprises: the golf course administration and, finally, the farm were all under the Moreton Enterprises umbrella and, a little later, the Sixth Form club.

Then there was Moreton Travel under the direction of David Lloyd which operated a British Rail Ticket Office with a turnover rising to £250,000. You could book for air travel, for ferries or for the Channel tunnel and for one purchaser a ticket from Heathrow to Australia via Cape Town was negotiated at minimum cost. Sir Bob Reid, head of British Rail, remarked that he only wished his organisation could show the profitability of Moreton Travel. Quality of Service certificates were presented by British Rail.

All this had led to interest and research into the re-opening or construction of local railway stations, though this initiative became somewhat bogged

Moreton Hall Travel.

down when local authorities and other bodies joined in. But the outstanding event which caused nationwide publicity was the taking over of Gobowen station where British Rail were making a heavy loss. This was run by the girls, with assistance, for two years 1993–95 and was not only a financial success but also a propaganda success for Moreton. Turnover more than doubled the British Rail figures.

This wide area of activity gave many girls a business experience which was unusual if not unique in schools. The down side was that if girls were to be given real responsibility it would also mean that they were free to make real mistakes; thus does one learn. But mistakes translated into finances could have awkward consequences. John Knight, looking at the accounts, had flashed a number of warning lights and in 1994 it was decided to appoint an Enterprise Manager not only to supervise the whole field but also to play a part in the school's accounting system. Mrs Susan Hill was appointed, herself an accountant and experienced in business. Moreton Services Ltd was set up to gather all the various enterprises under one head and generally a more rigorous approach was adopted, Susan Hill stayed for four years before going to pursue her own business interests and did much to establish a tighter accounting system, with monthly checks, not only for Moreton Enterprises but also for the school's accounts. In fact her title was changed to Bursar. A re-constituted Governors' Finance Committee with Derek Edwards in the chair – he was most active in Moreton affairs and generous with his time – was set up and Susan Hill with the Committee and the Principal produced an annual budget, John Knight, after many years of service, becoming a consultant. One area in which Susan Hill was active was that of holiday letting which became a useful source of subsidiary income. Another side of the school which was closely examined and re-ordered was that of maintenance and the work of the permanent staff employed. Roger Goolden retired in 1993; he had been Clerk of Works since 1963 – 'Mr Fixit' to whom everyone had turned when there was a practical job to be done.

Perhaps the most important sphere to which the Principal devoted a great deal of attention was that of pastoral care, seeking – and successfully seeking – (though it took time) to change the general staff attitude. As he told his Governors when he arrived, pastoral care for the whole school was in the hands of twelve female staff – Housemistresses who taught, Housemistresses who did not teach and Matrons. There was a divide between the teachers and the carers, whom some at any rate thought had inferior jobs. Jonathan Forster was determined to reverse this situation totally. If you taught at Moreton your work did not end in the form room. Every girl in future was not only going to be in a House but also in a Tutor Group with as many members of staff as possible acting as tutors, thus establishing personal relationships with small groups. There were inducements and allowances for those who carried extra responsibilities. Resident and non-resident alike, the staff were drawn into the complete life of the boarding school. Better accommodation was provided for Housemistresses whose general status was both enhanced and rewarded. In addition, staff were encouraged in the leading and supervision of extra-curricular activities on a much greater scale than before.

To add another strand to the pastoral network, a scheme was started whereby each Upper Sixth girl acted as mentor to a small group of younger girls. This idea was from the Sixth Form themselves and prevented the seniors from being too detached from the juniors.

The '90s saw the departure of some long serving members of the staff. In 1992 Judy Roe had retired after twenty-five years, distinguished not only for her teaching but for her capacity to take responsibility and her general calming influence. She was a person whom everyone trusted. Geoff and Pauline Norman also retired. It was seventeen years since the Governors had paid for them to make the long trip from Africa for interview; they had played very full parts in the life of the school. Trish Fenwick was another who would be hard to replace, particularly in her responsibility for the running of Norton-

Roberts, the province of the younger girls. And then, surpassing all, there was the retirement of Joan Pennington, now Mrs Franklin. To celebrate her fifty years at Moreton, a lunch party was given in her honour, during which she spoke of former times, of the days of djibbers and Cromwells, of Bronwen Lloyd-Williams and her habit, on a fine day, of sending the girls off to Wales for the fresh air with the parting injunction, 'Romp, girls, romp'; of iron bedsteads, thin mattresses and no carpets; of the cottages, barns and pig-sties where now more splendid buildings stand. Joan had been at the centre of school life for all these years, apparently able to absorb any amount of work, always placid, holding in her mind half a century of Moreton history. At much the same time,

Joan Franklin

another of the important figures in the schools history died – Ursula Roberts, who, sadly, did not live to a long retirement, so well earned. She had been a pupil back in the Loran House days in Oswestry with 'Aunt Lil'.

In 1994 Moreton underwent an inspection by OFSTED. It passed satisfactorily, the visitors noting the high levels of motivation and involvement by the pupils and appreciating that the quality of boarding life was high. 'The school has done much to achieve one of its aims: to provide a family atmosphere with care and concern shown to all its members. By comparison with national standards, most lessons seen were judged to be average or higher than average.' The girls certainly enjoyed the experience. 'After the

An informal tutorial.

initial shock and the realisation that some big, almighty inspector could be reading through my spelling mistakes, incomprehensible maths conclusions and the idiotic science solutions, the reality turned out to be far more pleasing. It was a bit like having an afternoon chat, biscuit in hand, with a vaguely exciting air of tension suspended around us. Great fun!' Whether the staff would describe the visit in such terms is more doubtful.

XII 'DOING FINE'

The school's eightieth birthday in 1993 was duly honoured; an Old Moretonian reunion was held and very well attended. The older generation found that the gym, where a service was held, was unrecognisable and had now become the Musgrave Centre. Although the School Psalm no longer featured, the School Prayers were the same as those with which Bronwen had brought to an end of many a long school day and Gaude Plebs was loudly sung. Denise Rylands spoke movingly of Doreen Cameron who had just died. As one visitor wrote, 'The flavour and atmosphere of Moreton is just the same; the girls are still poised, outgoing, dependable and just as ready to "entertain a stranger". But the pulse of the school seems to be beating faster now.'

When Mark Wright and David Lloyd left the staff, the activities of Moreton Enterprises were to some extent reined in. It was not possible to run Gobowen Station indefinitely; and some of the other activities had become just too time consuming. However the main functions of Moreton Enterprises continued and there was ample opportunity for girls to have real experience in the business world.

The need to have a modern, fully sophisticated IT centre had become more pressing. The Governors decided that an Appeal for this single object should be launched. Katie Neilson, who had become a Governor in 1995, was in the chair of the Appeal committee and threw herself with outstanding enthusiasm into the project. Various events were organised, the two most successful being a ball to mark the eighty-fifth anniversary, and an auction. The Appeal finally raised nearly £300,000 and the new centre, opened in 2000, was ultimately to

Thea Musgrave

provide for the use of 160 computers; the whole school was networked and IT became a compulsory study for all up to GCSE level. The new centre was rightly named the Neilson Centre.

To the eternal problem of what was there to do at weekends, Jonathan Forster had his own solution. Instead of the complicated rules concerning exeats and who could have them and for how long, he decided that girls could go out on any week-end. But for those who couldn't or didn't want to there were things going on – obviously sport for the sport minded but now also music and art and drama and there was generally a play in rehearsal: there was the computer centre for IT enthusiasts; golf for golfers: and generally some sort of entertainment. No longer were the weekend hours long and boring. Also it is important to mention that twinning between Moreton and Shrewsbury School Houses led to recreational activities which mostly took place on Saturdays. In 1995 – which saw a splendid production of the Mikado – Moreton for the first time ventured to the Edinburgh Fringe with a rock musical Cinderella: a successful experience, to be repeated.

By the beginning of the twenty-first century Jonathan Forster had a very committed staff, led by Mike Hartley as Deputy Head (Academic) and Paul Warren, Deputy Head (Extended Curriculum). Paul also ran the Duke of Edinburgh awards –more than forty girls on their way to achieving Gold in 2000. The improvement in academic results was really remarkable, giving the lie forever to the saying that Moreton was not an academic school. In 2001 at 'A' level, thirty-five per cent of the entrants obtained A grades and eighty-four per cent obtained A to C grades. By comparison the figure in 1990 had been fifty-three per cent. Five girls were accepted at Oxford or Cambridge in 2002. Passes in GCSE were now as of routine around ninety-eight per cent. Moreton Hall could now look any of her competitors fully in the face and compare with the country's best. Taking 'A' level points-per-subject as a measurement, in 2002 figures locally were Shrewsbury School 103, Shrewsbury High School 103, Moreton Hall 101. Moreton's GCSE results were the best of these three schools.

Needless to say, none of this was achieved without hard work by pupils and staff. Staff training and staff appraisal had been introduced and the timetable has again been overhauled and more use made of Saturday mornings, introduced with such hesitation by Jim Cussell fifteen years before. The aim was to have no class of more than fifteen girls; the consequence of this was, naturally a high staffing ratio, particularly if the needs of coaching for the Oxbridge candidates was considered; and if the school was going to provide, as it did, a multitude of out of school activities, as well as aid for the dyslexic and others who might need special care. Thus there was an endless tug of war between the need to economise and the need for the school to fulfil and indeed excel over a wide range. Accountants shake their heads over the high staff costs (seventy per cent of income) but were not the very reasons for parents choosing Moreton bound up with the range of activities coupled with the high academic standards which demanded a large staff?

Jonathan and Paula Forster.

The question of numbers was never absent from discussion and, at times, anxiety. The plain fact was that the number of girls boarding in the country had fallen by fifty per cent in ten years. It was really a triumph that numbers had kept up and indeed increased in Jonathan Forster's time. His own recruiting activities had much to do with this. Whereas in Bronwen's day, Governors had worried that the percentage of overseas girls was too high, in more recent years they worried that they were too low and that the international character of the school, which had been part of Bronwen's legacy, had largely disappeared.

Accordingly Jonathan Forster looked far afield. Overseas visits by himself to Spain, to Germany, to Singapore, to Australia and particularly to China brought in girls from all these places, both nationals and daughters of expatriates. Europe and the Far East were now the recruiting grounds whereas Bronwen's links had been with the Middle East and Africa. The other new source was the creation of Moreton First to cater for girls below the age of eleven. Whereas the old Transitional form had died a dozen years before, this new enterprise took off immediately and had a roll of fourteen in its first year. In addition improved transport arrangements made it more possible for day girls to enter fully into school life together with the availability of beds for brief overnight stays if required by family circumstances. Thus did Moreton defy the national tendency as regards girl boarders. In the ninetieth birthday year there are 301 in the school.

At the end of the century certain well-known figures retired from the Moreton scene. Keith and Dorothy Hunter brought their long innings to a close: 'Uncle Bob' Knill left after thirty-two years having occupied a central place in school life as did Les Cadwallader who had made a huge contribution together with his wife Effie. John Knight retired from the position of auditor, a job he had been doing for so long that the actual date is lost in the mists of time. There was a Memorial Service for Jim Cussell in 2001 to which came his children and their families. The Address was given by Evelyn Davies, and there was an attendance of about 150 – former staff, former pupils and friends from far and near.

So why do parents send their daughters to Moreton Hall? They know that there is a high standard of academic teaching; but what else? What is the meaning of the oft repeated cliché 'value added'? There are of course the activities to be found in most boarding schools. Drama has been particularly flourishing in recent years with another visit to the Edinburgh fringe with Oh What a Lovely War and in the same year a junior performance of The Tempest. (And what school has a dress room containing 4000 items?) Music was less prominent owing to staff changes but is now in the ascendant. In sport the fine lacrosse record has been maintained and sharply raised by having an English international on the staff; there are well organised teams in swimming, hockey, netball, badminton, rounders, cross-country, cricket – and even football.

What outside these normal activities does Moreton provide? Not many schools have a well equipped recording studio, even fewer no doubt a radio station. RK1 broadcasting on FM 87.7 to the campus and surrounding area was the brainchild of Rachel Porter and Katherine Sentance and programmes are put together on most days. (They were delighted to receive a letter form some inhabitants of Weston Rhyn who enjoyed listening.)

As in the days of 'Aunt Lil' and her Lloyd-Williams successors there is the

Miss Newcombe in the coveted GB vest.

traditional training in spoken English, with many successes in examination and competitions run by the English Speaking Board and others; and the emphasis on good manners and social skills continues.

Then there is Moreton Enterprises, now housed in its own business centre, in its size and scope almost certainly unique in either girls or boys schools. Enterprises today has divisions for tuck shop, stationery, horticulture, bank, (throughput of £60,000 a year) and transport, each with its divisional manager

The recording studio.

and assistants (also a Coke manager selling up to 1500 litres a year, and a chocolate manager, consumption not stated): the whole under central control with directors, officers and shareholders. All these enterprises are run by the girls themselves with the minimum of adult supervision. This is serious work experience, generally superior to that which is on offer outside the campus. Moreton has figured prominently in national Young Enterprises Awards.

Thus does Young Enterprise flourish. But what of Old Enterprise, the Governing Council? Year in, year out, the Governors have to make the key decisions – on expenditure, on the size of the fees, on the salary scale and on schemes brought to them by the Principal. There are many men and women, not mentioned in this narrative, who have given freely of their time and talent to the school, rewarded only by a satisfying lunch. It must be said to the Council's credit that the only two occasions when they had to make decisions vital to the future, they got the right answers in the appointment of Jim Cussell and of Jonathan Forster. Except on these two occasions, the Governors have never thought of themselves as executives, a mistake which has been made in some schools. Governors should take to heart the definition of the powers of monarchy in Victoria's reign by the historian Bagehot – the right to be informed, to advise and to warn.

It has not been easy in the past, nor will it be in the future, to get the balance between income and expenditure right when income depends on numbers which may fluctuate considerably. The bank too has to be kept happy; it has sometimes not been so. The school has been fortunate to have had and still to have, Malcolm Mitchell as Chairman, a man with wide experience of schools and, while recognising that running a school is a business, knows well that there are areas and qualities in school life which never appear on a balance sheet. At this time too, it is appropriate to salute three Governors who have been members from the very beginning in 1964, when Bronwen asked some friends to sit around table and told them they were the Governing Council (though she did the governing) – John Marchant, Denise Rylands and Margaret Williams – now Mrs Job.

The new boarding house – Charlesworth House.

Encouraged by the progress – in every way – under Jonathan Forster the Governing Council, freed after many years from the burden of loan repayments, decided to undertake the erection of a new boarding house, Charlesworth House, which now, at the time of writing in the school's ninetieth year is being erected; at the same time a thorough re-ordering and decoration of much of the rest of the school is taking place. It has long been clear that the boarding accommodation was not up the high standards which are expected today. The new House will set new standards – every room will be en-suite, incidentally a most important matter when it comes to holiday letting. Having sixty girls thus accommodated, there is scope for re-planning the space vacated for the rest of the school. Thus have the Governors recorded a marked vote of confidence in Moreton's future.

What would 'Aunt Lil' and her daughters make of today's school? Of course they would be surprised but they surely would be proud of the standing of the school today. In 2002 the Sunday Times listed the 'Top 20 Boarding Schools' in the country, both boys' and girls': they ranked Moreton Hall as nineteenth. Yet despite the remarkable success which this figure illustrates, the Lloyd-Williams clan – the founding Mothers – would still find today that same family atmosphere which over sixty years they had tried so hard to establish and maintain. As they would have wished, today's girls are friendly, forthcoming and confident – a characteristic at once noticeable to visitors and which has been remarked on by various teams of Inspectors.

The Independent Schools Council's Inspectors visited the school in 2000. This is the overall summary:

> Moreton Hall is an excellent school. It provides a very good education for all its pupils. Pupils' performance is impressive across examinations, art, music, sport, in the Duke of Edinburgh scheme, and in the activities in Moreton Enterprises. Pupils make a significant contribution to the quality of life of this school community. The excellent relationships between staff and pupils and the mutual respect of pupils for each other are key factors in the success of this school. The boarding provision is of a very high quality and allied to the high quality teaching gives an all round experience of real value to all pupils. The leadership of the school is a significant element in the success of the school.

On a more informal note, here is the comment of the Good Schools Guide in 1998:

> Open and chatty girls. Jolly, friendly and uninstitutional. Unstuffy small boarding school in a rural area that teaches girls to stand firmly in their own feet and does not produce stereotypes. Doing fine.

INDEX